The
True History of
Shakespeare's Sonnets

The
True History of
Shakespeare's Sonnets

by

Lord Alfred Douglas

KENNIKAT PRESS
Port Washington, N. Y./London

TO
OLIVE

THE TRUE HISTORY OF SHAKESPEARE'S SONNETS

First published in 1933
Reissued in 1970 by Kennikat Press
Library of Congress Catalog Card No: 70-113364
ISBN 0-8046-1014-2

Manufactured by Taylor Publishing Company   Dallas, Texas

PREFACE

LET it not be counted to me for arrogance or impertinence that I here claim to have set forth the true story of Shakespeare's Sonnets for the first time. Nor let anyone suppose that I am importing into that story any fantastic or far-fetched theories of my own. The story of the Sonnets is there, as it always has been, staring the enquirer in the face. Commentator after commentator has glimpsed it, and hastily shyed off it. It stands out perfectly plainly from the text of the Sonnets illuminated by Thorpe's dedication to their 'onlie begetter, Mr. W.H.' All I have done is to piece it together and to put it into plain English; rescuing it on the one hand from commentators like Samuel Butler (who after unravelling the puzzle with consummate skill, proceeded to muddle it all up again, by what I can only describe as flat-footed stupidity), and on the other hand from would-be moralists like Hallam who found it 'impossible not to wish that Shakespeare had never written the Sonnets'.

I have imbedded the Sonnets in the text of this book instead of printing each separately on its own page, because one of my objects is to make the present generation read these incomparable poems; and if they read my book they will be forced to read the Sonnets, and to read them all.

Of the fact that very few, even among the most cultivated, really read the Sonnets (except perhaps about a dozen of the best known) I have been made aware by a lifetime of experience. One has only to quote a line from one of the less known Sonnets to find that ninety-nine times out of a hundred it is unrecognized.

Finally, to those good people, a solid phalanx, who while professing to admire the Sonnets as great poetry, declare that they are not interested in their story and that it really does not matter two pins to whom they were addressed, I oppose a sceptical smile. Either they are not honest, or they belong, whether they know it or not, to the Hallam school of criticism; for if they really appreciated the Sonnets for what in truth they are, the 'high-top gallant' of poetry, they would not insult their own or other people's intelligence by pretending indifference to their meaning and to the story which they tell. It is as though, being offered the 'Key' with which 'Shakespeare unlocked his heart', they were to reply, 'I am not interested in Shakespeare's heart and I would rather not have the key'. I find it difficult to suffer such people gladly.

NOTE ON PROSODY AND PRONUNCIATION

THE text of the Sonnets as printed in this book follows the Quarto exactly in the matter of capital letters and italics. I have also consistently elided vowels, where the scansion of the line demands it. There is a strange inconsistency in this respect in most editions of the Sonnets.

To take an example almost at random from the Temple edition. In Sonnet 29 the sixth line is printed as follows:

'Featured like him, like him with friends possess'd.'

Here the last 'e' is elided in the word 'possessed' but not in the word 'featured'. Obviously the 'e' should be elided in both cases, thus:

'Featur'd like him, like him with friends possess'd.'

There are dozens of similar inconsistencies in the Temple edition text, with the result that anyone reading any sonnet for the first time would not know whether to sound the 'e's' or not. In this book an 'e', or any other vowel, which is not elided, must always be pronounced. (I mean of course only where the question of sounding or eliding arises at all.)

e.g. Sonnet 137 (116 Q.), line 5.

'O, no! it is an ever fixed mark.'

Here of course, fixed=fixèd.

Again Sonnet 107 (86 Q.), line 8.

'Giving him aid, my verse astonished.'

astonished=astonishèd.

A perfectly legitimate way of printing lines like those I have quoted above would be to print all the 'e's' and mark with an accent those that are to be sounded.

e.g. 'Featured like him, like him with friends possessed.'
and 'O, no! it is an ever fixèd mark.'

vii

It does not matter at all which method is adopted, but once the method *is* adopted it must be consistently followed if confusion is to be avoided.

The word 'even' is sometimes used in the sonnets as two syllables and sometimes as one. In the latter case it might be spelt 'e'en'.

e.g. Sonnet 92 (71 Q).

'But let your love e'en with my life decay.'

I have however left it as 'even' in every case.

NOTE ON THE FRONTISPIECE

THE portrait which appears as a frontispiece to this book is reproduced by the kind permission of the John Rylands Librarian at Manchester. It is known as the 'Grafton Portrait'. It has been conjectured that it might be a portrait of Shakespeare at the age of twenty-four. Mr. Dover Wilson in his brilliant book, *The Essential Shakespeare*, writes about it as follows:

'As the inscription at the top shows, he (the young man in the portrait) was Shakespeare's exact contemporary, and a comparison with the Droeshout engraving reveals the further coincidence that the relative distances from the chin to the lower lip, from the lower lip to the tip of the nose, from the tip of the nose to the lower eyelid, from the lower eyelid to the eyebrow, and from the eyebrow to the top of the forehead are identical in both portraits.'

The Droeshout engraving was, of course, done from the bust at Stratford which is believed to have been modelled from the death-mask of Shakespeare.

MR. J. M. ROBERTSON

As Mr. J. M. Robertson is criticised in this book, it seems advisable to state that his regretted death occurred while the book was actually in the press.

PART ONE

The Sonnets of Shakespeare were first published in quarto in 1609. The Title page of this edition (which was entered in the Stationers' Register on May 20th, 1609) runs as follows:

Shake-Speares
Sonnets
never before Imprinted

———

At London.

By G. Eld for T.T. and are to be solde by John Wright, dwelling at Christ Church Gate.

1609.

The well-known dedication from T.T. (Thomas Thorpe), the publisher, to Mr. W.H., the 'onlie begetter' of the sonnets, reads:

TO.THE.ONLIE.BEGETTER.OF
THESE.INSUING.SONNETS.
MR.W.H.ALL.HAPPINESS.
AND.THAT.ETERNITIE.
PROMISED.
BY.
OUR.EVER.LIVING.POET
WISHETH
THE.WELL-WISHING.
ANDVENTURER.IN
SETTING.
FORTH.

T.T.

The identity of 'T.T.' as Thomas Thorpe is established by the entry in the Stationers' Register, referred to above, where his name is given in full.

Two of the sonnets, those numbered in the Quarto edition 138 and 144, had already appeared in 'The Passionate Pilgrim' published by Jaggard in 1599; the remaining 152 were published for the first time in Thomas Thorpe's edition.

Samuel Butler points out that this slight deviation from the literal accuracy of the statement made on Thorpe's title-page that the sonnets had never been printed before, leaves us at liberty to hold that though Mr. W.H. is declared by Thorpe to be 'the onlie begetter' of the insuing sonnets, some few of them may not have been begotten by him, though he was the begetter of by far the greater number.

No further edition of the Sonnets appeared till 1640 when J. Benson published a collection entitled *Poems: Written by Will Shakespeare, Gent.* which contained all but eight of the sonnets as well as 'A Lover's complaint'. Benson puts inept headings of his own to arbitrarily selected groups of the sonnets and he went so far as to change 'he' and 'his' into 'she' and 'her' in some of them!

In his preface he refers to these 'excellent and sweetely composed Poems of Master William Shakespeare, which in themselves appear of the same purity as the authour himself then living avouched; they had not the fortune by reason of their infancie in his death to have the due accommodation of proportionable glory with the rest of his ever-living Works, yet the lines themselves will afford you a more authentic approbation than my assurance any way can, to invite your allowance.'

Shakespeare had been dead twenty-four years when Benson's mutilated and bowdlerised edition appeared, and it practically held the field till Malone's supplement to Johnson's edition of the plays appeared in 1780, after which date and down to the present day the Sonnets have been reprinted over and over again with varying emendations, as they originally appeared in the quarto edition of Thorpe. The only exception to this almost universal reproduction of Benson's barbarities down to Malone's edition in 1780, is Lintott's publication of the whole of Shakespeare's Poems about 1709. Here the sonnets are imprinted in the order given in the quarto. On the title page of this edition the Sonnets are declared to be all in praise of 'Shakespeare's Mistress'! The absurdity of this statement needs no pointing out, and it has been throughout the ages the fate of these sonnets to inspire ludicrous and self-evident absurdities among their commentators.

I cannot find that Benson's statement that Shakespeare 'avouched the purity' of the Sonnets has been sufficiently considered. To me it seems of profound importance. Obviously, Benson could not be intending to mean that Shakespeare had avouched the purity of the text of his (Benson's) version of the Sonnets. Benson deliberately falsified the text, presumably because he thought that the great majority of the sonnets being addressed to a boy, would be held to imply something immoral or disreputable; yet he declares, only twenty-four years after Shakespeare's death, at a time when many who knew Shakespeare personally and intimately would be still alive and aware of the circumstances attending the first publication of the Sonnets in 1609, that Shakespeare defended their 'purity'. Patently, then, he means that Shakespeare defended the Sonnets from the imputation of impurity or immorality which has been attached to them not only by Samuel Butler who deliberately argues that such impurity is inevitably to be deduced from them, but implicitly also by almost the entire mass of the other commentators, from Chalmers right down to Mr. J. M. Robertson, who by trying to explain them away, and by protesting against the acceptance of their plain significance, no less than Butler do Shakespeare the worst injury.

It is, nevertheless, true that, except for one fatal blemish, Samuel Butler's *Reconsideration* of the Sonnets (published 1899) is the most valuable and honest book that has ever been written on the subject.

He makes the most complete hay of the Pembroke and Southampton theories. He shows quite conclusively that 'Master W.H.' (Master not 'Mister' please) could not possibly have been either the Earl of Pembroke or the Earl of Southampton. Quite apart from his theory for which he makes out a convincing case, that Shakespeare wrote the Sonnets when he was between the ages of twenty-one and twenty-four when Pembroke and Southampton were both 'in the nursery', he shows that the assumption that the 'begetter' or inspirer of the Sonnets was Shakespeare's patron, or a wealthy nobleman, is utterly unsupported by the text of the Sonnets and is indeed plainly refuted there, and he leads his readers back to the truth which is as nearly obvious as anything which is sometimes disputed can be said to be; namely that the youth to whom Shakespeare addressed the greater part of the Sonnets was one William Hughes (or Hews as the name would indifferently have been spelt).

In justice to Oscar Wilde it must be pointed out that he made all these points ten years before Butler.

I must confess that for many years, not having gone

into the question, and having been content to take my views about Shakespeare's life from accredited 'Shakespearian Scholars' like the late Sir Sydney Lee (who is beautifully carved up in Butler's *Reconsideration*), I was under the impression that it was Oscar Wilde who first suggested that Master W.H. was Will (or as Wilde maddeningly insists upon calling him 'Willie') Hughes. It was only about fifteen years ago, when I happened to light on a jocular reference to 'another case of Master Will Hughes' in one of Byron's letters, that I realized that Wilde was not the inventor of the theory, and I must add that he, rather disingenuously, omits all mention in his story 'The portrait of Mr. W. H.', of Tyrwhitt who was the first to conjecture that W.H. stood for Will Hughes, or of other commentators who have at least noticed the conjecture though they unanimously reject it.

Tyrwhitt whose conjecture is endorsed and approved by Malone, to whom it was made and who incorporated it in his 1780 edition of *The Poems of Shakespeare*, founded his conjecture on the sonnets 135, 136 and 143 where the poet puns on the name 'Will' and on the 20th sonnet where the line

'A man in hew all *Hews* in his controlling'
gives the key to his friend's surname.

Malone says: 'Mr. Tyrwhitt has pointed out to me a

16

line in the twentieth sonnet which inclines me to think
that the initials W.H. stand for William Hughes.
Speaking of this person the poet says:

'A man in *hew* all *Hews* in his controlling.'
So the line is exhibited in the old copy.

(The name Hughes was formerly written Hews.)
When it is considered that one of these sonnets is
formed entirely on a play on our author's Christian
name, this conjecture does not seem improbable. To
this person, whoever he was, 120 of the following
poems are addressed. The remaining twenty-eight are
to a lady.'

Butler points out that there are three mistakes in
this paragraph. (1) In 'the old copy' the word 'hew' is
not in italics. It is only the word *Hews* which is
italicized. But this simply adds to the force of Tyrwhitt's conjecture. (2) There is a mistake as to the
number of sonnets addressed respectively to Mr.
W.H. and to the 'dark lady'. (3) The majority of the
last twenty-eight sonnets are obviously not written to
a woman.

But the mistakes in Malone's paragraph pointed out
by Butler do not affect the fact that Malone adopted
Tyrwhitt's conjecture, and anyone who reads the Sonnets freshly, with an open mind and with a determination not to 'shy off' from anything which he does not

THE TRUE HISTORY OF

approve, will, I venture to say, almost certainly come to the same conclusion.

Now Wilde in 1889, ten years before Butler wrote his book, adopted, or rather appropriated, Tyrwhitt's and Malone's conjecture. That Butler in 1889 did not acknowledge Wilde as a precursor and that he ignored his very brilliant essay altogether, may have been due to the fact that he had not read 'The Picture of Mr. W.H.'. It had then only appeared in *Blackwood's Edinburgh Magazine* and had not been reprinted in book form. But I think it is far more likely that Butler had read it and that he omitted to mention Wilde because at that time (within four years of his conviction), nobody in England mentioned him if he could avoid it. Butler, although all his life in revolt against *l'hypocrisie Anglaise*, was no braver than the theatrical managers who took Wilde's name off the play-bills of his own plays. Moreover, the bringing up of Wilde's name in this particular connection might have been at that date very 'awkward' for Butler, just as I suppose it will be considered 'awkward' for the present writer who, however, having a perfectly clear conscience, and being, moreover, prepared to defend Shakespeare at all costs and risks, has long ceased to be influenced by such considerations.

To avoid misunderstanding it is necessary to emphasize that while Butler distinctly brings the charge of homosexualty against Shakespeare on the evidence of the Sonnets, Wilde in 'The Portrait of Mr. W.H.' refrains from doing anything of the kind, and in a passage in 'Dorian Gray' by implication definitely rejects it.

The present writer, while accepting it as perfectly obvious and indisputable that the great majority of Shakespeare's incomparable Sonnets (which comprise among them the finest poetry that has ever been written in this or any language) were written to, or about, a boy whom Shakespeare adored, utterly rejects the notion that Shakespeare was a homosexualist. That this is not a thesis artificially trumped up to cover the exigences of the moment or to make it a little less difficult to write and publish this short essay, is easy to prove.

As long ago as 1921, when I was editing *Plain English*, I wrote an article in that weekly journal called 'Slinging Mud at Shakespeare', in which I defended Shakespeare against this charge, and against other foul-mouthed aspersions of the unspeakable Frank Harris and his admirers, among whom the late Arnold Bennett was conspicuous. (Bennett distinguished himself by declaring that Harris's fantastic imbecilities in 'The Man Shakespeare' had 'destroyed nearly all previous criticism and will be the parent of nearly all the Shakespearian criticism of the future'.)

Eight years later I touched on the subject again in my Autobiography (published 1929), and as what I then wrote contains the gist of what I now wish to repeat and emphasize on this point, I am reproducing it here. I was referring to certain letters written by Wilde.

'The language he used was of course extravagant and unusual. But there is nothing whatever in his letters which could not be matched in Shakespeare's sonnets (also written to a boy), and though I believe it is the fashion nowadays to accuse Shakespeare of having had the same vices as Wilde, this merely shows the ignorance and baseness and stupidity of those who make such accusations on such grounds. Shakespeare, as I have pointed out before, refuted his detractors, by anticipation, in the last six lines of the very sonnet which is generally quoted as the strongest evidence against him. I refer to the sonnet beginning:

'A woman's face with Nature's own hand painted,
Hast thou, the Master-Mistress of my passion.'

'The lines enumerated above (that is to say the last

six lines) clearly show, not only that Shakespeare's passion for "Mr. W.H." was perfectly innocent, but that Shakespeare himself had never envisaged the possibility of its being anything else. "Nature", says he, who intended thee for a woman "fell a-doting" and "by addition, me of thee defeated." Could anything be clearer? "If you had been a woman . . . but unfortunately you were a boy, so that I was defeated." To rub it in still more strongly he goes on to say:

'But since she prick'd thee out for woman's pleasure, Mine be thy love, and thy love's use their treasure.'

'(Observe here the tremendous force of the antithesis between "thy love" and "thy love's use".)

'The effect of the lines referred to is even stronger because they are so obviously not deliberately made in answer to, or in anticipation of, any adverse suggestion. Shakespeare exculpates himself, in the eyes of any reasonable being, quite definitely and quite unconsciously. Obviously it never occurred to him that anyone would put a bad interpretation on his love and adoration for "Mr. W.H.".'

That concludes the extract from my Autobiography and I now reproduce the sonnet in question in full.

A woman's face. with Nature's own hand painted,
Hast thou the master-mistress of my passion;
A woman's gentle heart, but not acquainted
With shifting change as is false woman's fashion
An eye more bright than theirs, less false in rolling,
Gilding the object whereupon it gazeth;
A man in hue, all *Hues* in his controlling,
Which steals men's eyes and women's souls amazeth.
And for a woman wert thou first created,
Till Nature as she wrought thee fell a-doting,
And by addition me of thee defeated
By adding one thing to my purpose nothing;
But since she prick'd thee out for woman's pleasure,
Mine be thy love and thy love's use their treasure.

It is the almost incredible fact that this beautiful sonnet is altogether omitted from Palgrave's edition of the Sonnets, which supports my contention that it is generally considered to be the 'strongest evidence' against Shakespeare. Palgrave in his 'Notes' at the end of the volume, which is called *Songs and Sonnets by William Shakespeare*, quotes Hallam as follows:

'There is a weakness and folly in all excessive and misplaced affection which is not redeemed by the touches of nobler sentiments that abound in this long series of sonnets. It is impossible not to wish that Shakespeare had never written them.'

Paraphrasing a remark of Orlando in *As You like It*, Shakespeare might retort 'There was no thought of pleasing you when they were written.'

A friend to whom I developed, in conversation, the thesis I have here propounded as to the overwhelming evidence for Shakespeare's innocence in this regard (which is supported by his passionate love of chastity and purity exemplified in the characters of all his heroines, and his hatred and contempt for what would now be considered by many people to be quite venial departures from that standard) said to me: 'Why should you be so anxious to acquit Shakespeare of homosexuality? Supposing he had been a homosexualist, would you have thought any worse of his poetry or his genius? Why get so excited because some people arrive at what appears to them to be a natural conclusion from his own written words?' To which I replied, as I do now, that if it could be proved that Shakespeare was a homosexualist, it certainly would not invalidate my admiration of his poetry, nor would I consider myself qualified to condemn him or to cast stones at him; but if the accusation (or the inference) is not true, and if there really is no evidence at all that he was a homosexualist, and if all the available evidence, such as it is, points utterly against it, why should he be libelled and defamed merely to gratify those who really are tarred with that brush on the one hand, and fools and prudes like Hallam on the other?

Any honest man who has been at a public school or a university must know perfectly well that young men and boys are liable to fall in love with other young men and boys, and they must also know equally well that some of these relationships are innocent and some are not. In cases where it becomes the legitimate business of any individual to find out into which of the two categories such a state of affairs falls, it is merely a matter of evidence. If Shakespeare is to be convicted of homosexuality on the evidence of his sonnets to Mr. W.H., then David, the Psalmist, who is venerated by Catholics as a Saint and one of the precursors of Christ, must be equally convicted on the strength of his lament for Jonathan. Would anyone in his senses make such a contention, unless he were an 'eminent counsel' speaking from a brief?

Here the development of my argument makes it necessary to quote in full three of the sonnets. The first is the one numbered 129 in the Quarto.

Butler, for whose opinion I have the greatest respect, cuts it right out of the series, labels it 'Appendix B' and describes it as 'An occasional Sonnet, probably given, but not addressed to Mr. W.H., nor in any way referring to him.'

The expense of Spirit in a waste of shame
Is lust in action; and till action, lust
Is perjur'd, murd'rous, bloody, full of blame,
Savage, extreme, rude, cruel, not to trust;
Enjoy'd no sooner but despised straight;
Past reason hunted; and no sooner had,
Past reason hated, as a swallow'd bait,
On purpose laid to make the taker mad:
Mad in pursuit, and in possession so;
Mad, having, and in quest to have extreme;
A bliss in proof, and prov'd, a very woe;
Before, a joy propos'd; behind, a dream.
    All this the world well knows, yet none knows well
    To shun the heaven that leads men to this hell.

I agree that this sonnet is not addressed to and has no reference to Mr. W.H., but I think it has a very distinct reference to the 'Dark Woman' who was Shakespeare's mistress but certainly not, as Yahoo Harris has called her, 'Shakespeare's Love'. It is numbered 129 in the Quarto and it comes between two sonnets which are plainly addressed to the 'Dark Woman', the first (128) a pleasing, conventional trifle in which the poet envies the 'Jacks' or notes which her fingers touch when she is playing the stringed instrument of the period which most nearly corresponds to the harpsichord, and the second (130), which I now quote in full, in which he gives his real opinion about this lady and her 'charms'.

My Mistress' eyes are nothing like the sun;
Coral is far more red than her lips red;
If snow be white, why then her breasts are dun;
If hairs be wire, black wires grow on her head.
I have seen Roses damask'd, red and white,
But no such Roses see I in her cheeks;
And in some perfumes is there more delight
Than in the breath that from my Mistress reeks.
I love to hear her speak, yet, well I know
That music hath a far more pleasing sound.
I grant, I never saw a goddess go,
My Mistress when she walks treads on the ground;
   And yet, by heaven, I think my love as rare
   As any she belied with false compare.

Butler euphemistically describes this sonnet thus: 'Concerning Shakespeare's Mistress. A satire on the amatory sonnets of the time.' Taken in conjunction with the sonnets about the 'jacks' and the sonnet about 'lust in action' which precede it in the Quarto, who can doubt that all three are in their right places in the series, and that they represent Shakespeare's true feelings about the 'Dark Lady' (who according to a recent writer in a literary paper was his 'inspiration' for Juliet, Imogen, Rosalind and all his heroines!) before and after that 'expense of spirit' which he so bemoans?

I think that fierce, terrible and devastating attack on 'lust in action', which is entirely in keeping with all Shakespeare's views on the subject whenever he is in his plays speaking seriously and from his heart, is an overwhelming proof of the innocence of his love for Mr. W.H. when it is put side by side with the following sonnet, 144 in the Quarto.

Two loves I have of comfort and despair
Which like two spirits do suggest me still:
The better angel is a man right fair,
The worser spirit a woman colour'd ill.
To win me soon to hell, my female evil
Tempteth my better angel from my side,
And would corrupt my saint to be a devil,
Wooing his purity with her foul pride.
And whether that my angel be turned fiend
Suspect I may, but not directly tell;
But being both from me, both to each friend,

I guess one angel in another's hell:
Yet this shall I ne'er know, but live in doubt,
Till my bad angel fire my good one out.

If this does not mean plainly that Shakespeare was 'in love' (in a perfectly innocent way) with a man or boy and was also carrying on an 'affair' with a woman whom, in spite of her deplorable 'sex-appeal', he despised and regarded as a 'devil' and an 'evil', and who was endeavouring to corrupt his innocent young friend, his 'saint', then it means nothing at all.

The truth is, in spite of Frank Harris and Arnold Bennett and all the other frantic worshippers at the shrine of what they are pleased to call 'the plain facts of life', that Shakespeare was a good deal of a puritan. He was almost certainly brought up a Catholic, and though he undoubtedly succumbed to the pressure of the times in which he lived and outwardly abandoned his religion, he never lost the Catholic view about purity and impurity. Doubtless he had mistresses, we know at any rate that he had one, 'the dark woman (why call her a lady?) of the Sonnets', but he had no romantic feelings about her or about any other woman of easy virtue. All his heroines, with the solitary exception of Cleopatra, were chaste and pure and lovely, and he could not take a 'charitable view' even about Cressida in these regards.

On the other hand he openly adored Mr. W.H. and celebrated his adoration in the most perfect poetry. *Honi soit qui mal y pense.*

The question now arises, who was Mr. W.H.? He was certainly not Pembroke, nor Southampton. He was, I believe, with Malone and Tyrwhitt and Butler, a youth called William Hughes. From the Sonnets we gather that he was very young, probably about eighteen or less when the Sonnets began, and about twenty or twenty-one when they petered out. He was very beautiful but neither of high birth nor of exalted position. Shakespeare began by imploring him in the first seventeen sonnets to marry and have children so that his beauty might be perpetuated in his offspring. (This, by the way, is surely an additional argument, if any more are needed, against the attempt to tar Shakespeare with a homosexual brush.) The remaining sonnets tell a story of continued adoration, broken by occasional complaints and the record of tiffs and reconciliations, until they come to the 'dark woman' episode which according to the commonly accepted idea wrecked the romantic friendship between the poet and his boy friend; the generally accepted version being that Mr. W.H. stole Shakespeare's mistress from him.

But anyone who takes the trouble to read the Sonnets for himself (and how many people really do read carefully any but the few greatest?) will soon perceive that the 'dark woman' affair was a very mild storm in a teacup. So far from the episode having broken up the friendship between Shakespeare and Mr. W.H., it appears quite plainly that Shakespeare had very little resentment about it. He forgave Mr. W.H. at once and even admitted that he was partly to blame for what had happened. Butler even suggests that he deliberately handed over his mistress to his young friend because he thought that it would be a good thing for him to have an 'affair' with a woman. I reject this theory as fantastic and quite in opposition to Shakespeare's views about purity and impurity, but I agree with Butler in his opinion that Thorpe, whether by accident or by design, disarranged the order of the Sonnets, and I take Butler's rearrangement of their order as a valuable piece of editing. Under Butler's arrangement the 'Story' of the Sonnets emerges in a much more coherent form, and the episode of the 'dark woman' falls into what I take to be its quite subsidiary place.

Instead of being among the last sonnets beginning at 127, the 'dark woman' episode begins after sonnet 39. Sonnet 127 in the Quarto begins the series con-

cerning the 'dark woman' and is numbered 40 by
Butler. Then follows 128 (Quarto) to which I have
already referred and which Butler numbers 41. He
then misses out (wrongly as I believe) 129 (Quarto)
and numbers 130 (Quarto) as 42. He omits other
sonnets which he puts in the appendix as 'occasional
poems', e.g. the one beginning:

'Oh thou my lovely Boy, who in thy power
Dost hold time's sickle, glass, his fickle hour,'

which, as he brilliantly suggests, was probably written
to be spoken to Mr. W.H. when acting the part of
Cupid in some mask. (This poem, I may point out,
is not a sonnet. It is simply a twelve-lined lyric written
in rhyming couplets. I think it's best place is where I
have put it, right at the beginning.)

The sonnet numbered 152 in the Quarto which, in
that edition, is the last referring to either Mr. W.H.
or the 'dark woman', and which therefore, until Butler's emendation of the order, had always been supposed
to be the sonnet which ended Shakespeare's connection
with Mr. W.H., is numbered 62 by Butler.

Thereafter, the 'dark woman' episode being finished,
the sonnets pursue their course until what Butler calls
'the final rupture' between Shakespeare and Mr. W.H.

comes at sonnet 148 (125 Q.) with the stinging couplet:

'Hence thou suborn'd *Informer!* a true soul
When most impeach'd stands least in thy control.'

Of this astonishing couplet, coming at the end of a sonnet which is full of love and humility, more anon when I come to deal with it in its place at the end of the series.

I am printing all the sonnets in the text of this book and I am commenting on them, sonnet by sonnet, where I think comment is necessary. For this purpose I am adopting Butler's rearrangement of the order except that, as already indicated, I retain the sonnet 'The expense of Spirit in a waste of shame' in its place in the rearranged order, whereas Butler takes it right out of the series and heads it 'Appendix B'. In the case of four other sonnets I have queried Butler's order and attribution to Mr. W.H., but I have tentatively left them as he placed and attributed them. I have not been able to make up my mind about them, and I await more light or inspiration about them.

Obviously it would be very easy for me to reproduce in other words the arguments by which Butler arrives at the new order in which he arranges the Sonnets; but as I am bound to admit that his rearrangement of the order never occurred to me independently, and as I am equally obliged to admit that until I saw them in his order I never had got anywhere near to understanding the story of the Sonnets, I think it is better simply to say that I accept and adopt Butler's arguments, in the main, both as to the approximate order in which the sonnets should be printed, and as to the age of Shakespeare (between twenty-one and twenty-four) when he wrote them. The points on which I differ from him will appear in their places in my comments on the sonnets.

Before starting my comments on the sonnets I must confess that until I had read Butler I had pretty nearly arrived at the conclusion that Oscar Wilde's theory (if it can be called his theory, for in his story he leaves the impression that he probably does not himself believe it) was the best that had ever been propounded.

Wilde's story, 'The Picture of Mr. W.H.', appeared in *Blackwood's Edinburgh Magazine* in July 1889, about two years before I first met him. I read the story about a year after I met him, and at that time he showed me a letter which he had received from Richard Garnett of the British Museum in which Garnett congratulated him very warmly on his 'brilliant piece of Shakespearian criticism' and said in effect, 'I more than half-believe that you have actually solved the secret of the Sonnets.'

Wilde's theory is so good and so ingenious that it is a thousand pities that he did not write it and put it forth as a theory and nothing else. Instead of this he wrapped round the theory what I can only describe as a very foolish and unconvincing story about a young man called Cyril Graham who causes a forged portrait of Will Hughes to be painted (and commits suicide to 'prove the truth' of the story he had evolved about Mr. W.H.), and his friend Erskine who, after first rejecting the story as absurd, afterwards becomes obsessed by it, and dies of consumption, leaving a letter to say that he also is committing suicide as a 'martyr' to the theory.

The result of all this silliness is that the excellence of the theory is obscured, and Wilde himself, as I have already said, leaves his readers in doubt as to whether he is really advancing a serious theory or simply indulging in a piece of clever 'leg-pulling'.

Wilde, however, did tell me more than once that he fully believed that his theory was correct, and at that time I did not know enough about the Sonnets (although I was constantly reading them as I have done all my life) to argue for or against his theory. It seemed to me convincing at the time, and I am glad to know that it appealed as strongly as it did to Richard Garnett who was a good Shakespearian scholar.

In fact, I was so enamoured of Wilde's theory that I am still rather reluctant to let it go altogether. But it is impossible to accept both Butler and Wilde because they are mutually contradictory on such points as the age of Shakespeare when he wrote the Sonnets (Wilde would make him much older, which, indeed, is the generally accepted idea), and the meaning of the sonnets in which Shakespeare complains about other poets who were also occupied with Mr. W.H. and his beauty.

I would have given a good deal to hear Wilde and Butler argue the matter out; but on the whole I think Butler is infinitely the more convincing, and that he had really gone into the whole question much more deeply than Wilde had done.

All the same, Wilde's theory is too good to be overlooked as it is now in danger of being overlooked.

I notice that my friend Mr. Augustus Ralli, whose recent monumental publication in two volumes, *A History of Shakespearian Criticism*, is positively indispensable to any serious student of Shakespeare, makes no mention at all either of Wilde or Butler.

Butler is in no danger of being neglected in this connection, but I have scarcely ever in recent years

met anyone who is conversant with Wilde's theory of
the Sonnets, and this is astonishing considering the
enormous vogue which he has enjoyed for the last
twenty years all over Europe.

Briefly, then, Wilde's theory is that Mr. W.H. was
Will Hughes (Wilde as I have said before calls him
'Willie') and that this Will Hughes was the boy actor
who 'created' most of Shakespeare's great female
parts, women being, of course, at that period debarred
from the stage and all female parts being played by
boys.

He demolishes the claims of Pembroke, as Butler
does, and as any intelligent reader of the Sonnets can
do for himself from Sonnet 25, among others, and he
adds the following:

'We know from Meres that the Sonnets had been
written before 1598, and Sonnet 104 informs us that
Shakespeare's friendship for Mr. W.H. had already
been in existence for three years. Now Lord Pembroke
who was born in 1580, did not come to London till
eighteen years of age, that is to say till 1598, and
Shakespeare's acquaintance with Mr. W.H. must have
begun about 1594, or at the latest 1595. Shakespeare
accordingly, could not have known Lord Pembroke
till after the Sonnets were written. Cyril pointed out

also that Pembroke's father did not die till 1601; whereas it was evident from the line

"You had a father, let your son say so,"

that the father of Mr. W. H. was dead in 1598.'

Regarding Southampton (whose claims are knocked out by Sonnet 25 just as completely as Pembroke's) Wilde has this:

'With Lord Southampton Cyril had even less difficulty. Southampton became at a very early age the lover of Elizabeth Vernon, so he needed no entreaties to marry; he was not beautiful, he did not resemble his mother, as Mr. W.H. did—

"Thou art thy mother's glass, and she in thee
Calls back the lovely April of her prime:"

and, above all, his christian name was Henry, whereas the punning sonnets (135 and 143) show that the Christian name of Shakespeare's friend was the same as his own—Will.'

'Cyril Graham' in the story goes on to develop his theory, and naturally he 'discovers' the surname

Hughes or Hews in the twentieth Sonnet. (This 'discovery' had, of course, been made more than a hundred years before, but Wilde, trusting to the general ignorance about the Sonnets, suppresses all mention of Tyrwhitt who first suggested the name.)

He (Cyril in the story) meets the objection that the name of Will Hughes does not occur in the list of the actors of Shakespeare's company as printed in the first folio, by pointing out that 'the absence of Willie Hughes's name from this list really corroborated the theory, as it was evident from Sonnet 86 that Willie Hughes had abandoned Shakespeare's company to play at a rival theatre, probably in some of Chapman's plays.

"But when your countenance filled up his line,
Then lacked I matter; that enfeebled mine." '

This seems to me to be rather brilliant, and later in the book Wilde, through 'Erskine', another character in his story, suggests that the rival dramatist here referred to might more probably be Marlowe and that the 'affable familiar ghost
        Which nightly gulls him with intelligence,'
was the Mephistopheles of his 'Doctor Faustus'.

Again I think that this is a brilliant conjecture. Wilde

is able to bolster up his theory by a number of aston-
ishingly apt and almost convincing quotations from
the Sonnets, for example:

'What is your substance, whereof are you made,
That millions of strange shadows on you tend?
Since every one hath, every one, one shade,
And you, but one, can every shadow lend.'

'Lines', he says, 'that would be unintelligible if they
were not addressed to an actor, for the word "shadow"
had in Shakespeare's day a technical meaning con-
nected with the stage. "The best in this kind are but
shadows", says Theseus of the actors in *Midsummer
Night's Dream*, and there are many similar allusions
in the literature of the day.'

Wilde's explanation of the meaning of the sonnets in
which Shakespeare implores Mr. W.H. to marry and
have children is the weakest part of his theory. It is
far-fetched and, I think, quite unconvincing. Nevertheless the very short indications I have given here of
his argument, which is supported by a mass of quotations from the Sonnets themselves, will serve, I hope,
to send students back to Wilde's story.

I do not know whether it has been published as a
book in England. My edition is a pirated American

one brought out by the late Mr. Mosher and acquired by me in or about the year 1907. The acceptance of Butler's theory does not altogether bar out that of Wilde. At least they both agree that the boy's name was Will Hughes, and he might well have been an actor. But if Butler is right about the date of the Sonnets, Will Hughes could not possibly be the boy who played Juliet and Viola and Imogen and Rosalind and Cleopatra, because none of the plays in which these characters appear was written till after the date which Butler fixes for the Sonnets. On the other hand, he may well have been an actor and have played the female parts in his company.

At any rate I would rather believe that Will Hughes was an actor than a *sea-cook*, which is the unromantic avocation which Butler (on quite hopelessly insufficient data) suggests for him!

On the whole, if I were constrained to pin myself down to a definite opinion as to the identity of the boy to whom Shakespeare addressed the great majority of his Sonnets, I would say with great confidence that his name was William Hughes, aged anything from sixteen to eighteen, and that he was an actor. If he was an actor it is perfectly certain that, at the age which I have conjectured for him, and with the appearance and smooth-cheeked beauty which Shakespeare ascribes to him, he would have acted the female parts in the plays produced by his company. This assumption leaves quite a considerable part of Wilde's theory alive and also fits in with the theory of Samuel Butler. I think that, between the two of them, they have got nearer to a solution than anyone else.

I now proceed to an examination of the Sonnets and I shall reinforce my argument as occasion arises.

PART TWO

Poem (not a sonnet) numbered 126 in the Quarto.
To Mr. W.H. (i.e., Master Will Hughes).

O Thou, my lovely boy, who in thy power
Dost hold Time's sickle, glass, his fickle hour;
Who hast by waning grown, and therein showest
Thy lovers with'ring as thy sweet self growest;
If Nature, sovereign mistress over wrack,   5
As thou go'st onwards still will pluck thee back,
She keeps thee to this purpose, that her skill
May time disgrace, and wretched minutes kill.
Yet fear her, O thou minion of her pleasure!
She may detain, but not still keep, her treasure: 10
Her Audit, though delay'd, answer'd must be,
And her quietus is to render thee.

Line 2. Quarto reads,
'Doest hould times fickle glasse, his sickle, hower.'
Many emendations have been proposed to this line
which is obviously corrupt. I have adopted Butler's

45

suggestion. This poem (it is not a sonnet but a twelve-lined lyric written in rhymed couplets) was probably written by Shakespeare to be spoken to Mr. W.H. when acting the part of Cupid in a mask. Butler prints it as 'Appendix A'. I have put it in front of all the sonnets to serve as a sort of Prologue. I venture to suggest (purely as a conjecture) that it may have been written by Shakespeare immediately after he first met Mr. W.H. I mean that he may have been asked or employed to write the lines and that this was the occasion of their first meeting. It goes some way to support Wilde's theory that Mr. W.H. was an actor.

I

To Mr. W.H. Urging him to marry and have children —so as to perpetuate the record of his beauty. *Spring* **1585.**

> From fairest creature we desire increase,
> That thereby beauty's *Rose* might never die,
> But as the riper should by time decease
> His tender heir might bear his memory:
> But thou, contracted to thine own bright eyes,   5
> Feed'st thy life's flame with self-substantial fuel,

Making a famine where abundance lies,
Thyself thy foe, to thy sweet self too cruel.
Thou that art now the world's fresh ornament
And only herald to the gaudy spring,   10
Within thine own bud buriest content
And, tender churl, mak'st waste in niggarding.
    Pity the world, or else this glutton be,
    To eat the world's due, by the grave and thee.

Line 6, Q. reads 'Feed'st thy light's flame.'
            The emendation is Butler's.
Butler dates this sonnet 'Spring 1585'. I accept this
date which would make Shakespeare just about
twenty-one when he wrote the sonnet.

2

To Mr. W.H., urging him to marry.

When forty winters shall besiege thy brow
And dig deep trenches in thy beauty's field,
Thy youth's proud livery, so gazed on now,
Will be a tatter'd weed, of small worth held:
Then being ask'd where all thy beauty lies,   5
Where all the treasure of thy lusty days,

47

To say, within thine own deep-sunken eyes,
Were an all-eating shame and thriftless praise,
How much more praise deserv'd thy beauty's use,
If thou couldst answer 'This fair child of mine   10
Shall sum my count and make my whole excuse',
Proving his beauty by succession thine.
   This were to be new made when thou art old,
   And see thy blood warm when thou feel'st it cold.

Line 4. 'Weed' here means 'garment'.
Line 11 reads 'Make my old excuse'.
   The emendation adopted here is Hazlitt's.
This sonnet clearly shows that Shakespeare, at the age
when he wrote it (about twenty-one as I conjecture),
looked upon a man (or woman) of forty as being completely worn out by old age. In Shakespeare's day a
boy would go to Oxford or Cambridge at twelve or
thirteen, be considered 'grown up' at eighteen, and
middle-aged at thirty. Butler acutely cites this sonnet
to support his theory that Shakespeare was very young
at the time he wrote it. To a young man of twenty-one
even to-day, forty seems to be a great age.

3

To Mr. W.H. urging him to marry.

Look in thy glass, and tell the face thou viewest,
Now is the time that face should form another,
Whose fresh repair if now thou not renewest,
Thou dost beguile the world, unbless some mother
For where is she so fair whose un-ear'd womb   5
Disdains the tillage of thy husbandry?
Or who is he so fond will be the tomb
Of his self-love, to stop posterity?
Thou art thy mother's glass, and she in thee
Calls back the lovely April of her prime: 10
So thou through windows of thine age shalt see,
Despite of wrinkles, this thy golden time.
    But if thou list remembr'd not to be
    Die single, and thine image dies with thee.

Line 5. 'Un-ear'd' means 'unploughed'.

Line 13, Q. reads 'But if thou live remembred not
to be', which makes no sense. Butler suggests 'list',
which brings out the obvious meaning of the last two
lines of the sonnet: 'If you want *not* to be remembered,
die single and without children to reproduce your
image.'

If Mr. W.H. were eighteen when this sonnet was
written, and if he had then married and had a son, he

would have been about thirty-seven when his son had reached the age of eighteen. Obviously, then, Shakespeare at this time looked upon thirty-seven as a time of 'wrinkles' and old age.

4

To Mr. W.H. urging him to marry.

Unthrifty loveliness, why dost thou spend
Upon thyself thy beauty's legacy?
Nature's bequest gives nothing, but doth lend,
And being frank, she lends to those are free.
Then, beauteous niggard, why dost thou abuse   5
The bounteous largess given thee to give?
Profitless usurer, why dost thou use
So great a sum of sums, yet canst not live?
For having traffic with thyself alone,
Thou of thyself thy sweet self dost deceive.   10
Then how, when nature calls thee to be gone,
What acceptable Audit canst thou leave?
   Thy unus'd beauty must be tomb'd with thee,
   Which, used, lives th' executor to be.

Line 12. Note that 'acceptable' to be scanned here must be pronounced with the accent on the first syllable, thus: àcceptable. Conf. *Romeo and Juliet*. *V, III*, 'Thou dètestable maw.'

5

To Mr. W.H. urging him to marry.

Those hours that with gentle work did frame
The lovely gaze where every eye doth dwell,
Will play the tyrants to the very same,
And that un-fair which fairly doth excel:
For never-resting time leads summer on   5
To hideous winter and confounds him there;
Sap check'd with frost and lusty leaves quite gone,
Beauty o'ersnow'd and bareness everywhere:
Then, were not summer's distillation left,
A liquid pris'ner pent in walls of glass,   10
Beauty's effect with beauty were bereft,
Nor it, nor no remembrance what it was:
    But flow'rs distill'd though they with winter meet,
    Leese but their show; their substance still lives
      sweet.

Line 1, Q. has 'Those howers' making the word two syllables, as is necessary to make the line scan.

Line 13, Q. has 'flowers' which is here used as one syllable as amended by me.

Line 14. Leese=lose (Chaucerian) as George Wyndham points out.

6

To Mr. W.H. urging him to marry.

Then let not winter's ragged hand deface
In thee thy summer, ere thou be distill'd:
Make sweet some vial; treasure thou some place
With beauty's treasure, ere it be self-kill'd.
That use is not forbidden usury   5
Which happies those that pay the willing loan;
That's for thyself to breed another thee,
Or ten times happier, be it ten for one;
Ten times thyself were happier than thou art,
If ten of thine ten times refigur'd thee: 10
Then what could death do, if thou shouldst depart,
Leaving thee living in posterity?
    Be not self-kill'd, for thou art much too fair
    To be death's conquest and make worms thine heir.

Line 13, Q. has 'self-will'd'. With Butler I adopt
the conjecture of Delius given in the Cambridge
edition.

7

To Mr. W.H. urging him to marry.

Lo, in the orient when the gracious light
Lifts up his burning head, each under eye

Doth homage to his new-appearing sight,
Serving with looks his sacred majesty;
And having climb'd the steep up-heavenly hill,　5
Resembling strong youth in his middle age,
Yet mortal looks adore his beauty still,
Attending on his golden pilgrimage;
But when from high-most pitch, with weary car,
Like feeble age, he reeleth from the day,　　　10
The eyes, 'fore duteous, now converted are
From his low tract, and look another way:
　　So thou, thyself outgoing in thy noon,
　　Unlook'd on di'st, unless thou get a son.

Line 5, Q. has no hyphen.　Malone reads 'steep-up
heavenly hill'.　I adopt Butler's version.

8

To Mr. W.H. urging him to marry.

Music to hear, why hear'st thou music sadly?
Sweets with sweets war not, joy delights in joy.
Why lov'st thou that which thou receiv'st not gladly,
Or else receiv'st with pleasure thine annoy?
If the true concord of well tuned sounds,　　5
By unions marri'd, do offend thine ear,
They do but sweetly chide thee, who confounds

In singleness the parts that thou shouldst bear.
Mark how one string, sweet husband to another,
Strikes each in each by mutual ordering; 10
Resembling sire and child and happy mother,
Who, all in one, one pleasing note do sing:
 Whose speechless song, being many, seeming one,
 Sings this to thee: 'Thou single wilt prove none'.

9

To Mr. W.H. urging him to marry.

Is it for fear to wet a widow's eye
That thou comsum'st thyself in single life?
Ah, if thou issueless shalt hap to die,
The world will wail thee, like a makeless wife;
The world will be thy widow, and still weep 5
That thou no form of thee hast left behind,
When every private widow well may keep
By children's eyes her husband's shape in mind.
Look, what an unthrift in the world doth spend
Shifts but its place, for still the world enjoys it; 10
But beauty's waste hath in the world an end,
And kept unus'd, the user so destroys it.
 No love toward others in that bosom sits
 That on himself such murd'rous shame commits.

Line 4, 'A makeless wife' = 'a mateless wife'.
Line 10, Q. reads 'shifts but his place'.

10

To Mr. W.H. urging him to marry.

For shame, deny that thou bear'st love to any,
Who for thyself art so unprovident.
Grant, if thou wilt, thou art belov'd of many,
But that thou none lov'st is most evident;
For thou art so possess'd with murd'rous hate   5
That 'gainst thyself thou stick'st not to conspire
Seeking that beauteous roof to ruinate,
Which to repair should be thy chief desire.
O, change thy thought, that I may change my mind!
Shall hate be fairer lodg'd than gentle love?   10
Be, as thy presence is, gracious and kind,
Or to thyself, at least, kind-hearted prove:
  Make thee another self, for love of me,
  That beauty still may live in thine or thee.

11

To Mr. W.H. urging him to marry.

As fast as thou shalt wane, so fast thou grow'st
In one of thine, from that which thou departest;
And that fresh blood which youngly thou bestow'st
Thou mayst call thine when thou from youth con-
    vertest.

Herein lives wisdom, beauty and increase;   5
Without this, folly, age and cold decay:
If all were minded so, the times should cease
And threescore year would make the world away.
Let those whom Nature hath not made for store,
Harsh, featureless and rude, barrenly perish: 10
Look whom she best endow'd she gave thee more;
Which bounteous gift thou shouldst in bounty
      cherish:
  She carv'd thee for her seal, and meant thereby
  Thou shouldst print more, not let that copy die.

Lines 1 and 2. The sense is: 'As fast as you grow older and your beauty wanes, so fast will your son who represents you grow to be like what you are now.'

Lines 2 and 4. Note that 'departest' is rhymed with 'convertest', so all through the Sonnets, time after time, 'ert' rhymes with 'art'. Conf. ' 'Varsity' as an abbreviation for 'University', 'Hertford' pronounced 'Hartford', etc. etc.

12

To Mr. W.H. urging him to marry.

When I do count the clock that tells the time,
And see the brave day sunk in hideous night;

When I behold the violet past prime,
And sable curls all silver'd o'er with white;
When lofty trees I see barren of leaves,
Which erst from heat did canopy the herd,
And summer's green all girded up in sheaves,
Borne on the bier with white and bristly beard;
Then of thy beauty do I question make,
That thou among the wastes of time must go,   10
Since sweets and beauties do themselves forsake,
And die as fast as they see others grow;
 And nothing 'gainst Time's scythe can make
  defence,
 Save breed, to brave him when he takes thee
  hence.

Line 4, Q. reads 'curls or silver'd ore'; the emendation adopted is Malone's.

.13

To Mr. W.H. urging him to marry.

O that you were yourself! but, love, you are
No longer yours than you yourself here live:
Against this coming end you should prepare,
And your sweet semblance to some other give.
So should that beauty which you hold in lease   5

Find no determination; then you were
Yourself again, after yourself's decease,
When your sweet issue your sweet form should bear.
Who lets so fair a house fall to decay,
Which husbandry in honour might uphold   10
Against the stormy gusts of winter's day
And barren rage of death's eternal cold?
 O, none but unthrifts: dear my love, you know
You had a Father; let your Son say so.

want him to have a child

14

To Mr. W.H. urging him to marry.

Not from the stars do I my judgement pluck;
And yet methinks I have Astronomy,
But not to tell of good or evil luck,
Of plagues, of dearths, or season's quality;
Nor can I fortune to brief minutes tell,   5
Pointing to each his thunder, rain and wind,
Or say with Princes if it shall go well,
By oft predict that I in heaven find:
But from thine eyes my knowledge I derive
And, constant stars, in them I read such art   10
As truth and beauty shall together thrive
If from thyself to store thou wouldst convert;
 Or else of thee this I prognosticate:
 Thy end is Truth's and Beauty's doom and date.

Line 8, 'predict' here is a substantive and='prediction'.

Lines 10 and 12. Note again 'art' rhymes with 'convert'.

15

To Mr. W. H. urging him to marry.

When I consider every thing that grows
Holds in perfection but a little moment,
That this huge stage presenteth nought but shows
Whereon the Stars in secret influence comment;
When I perceive that men as plants increase   5
Cheer'd and check'd even by the self-same sky,
Vaunt in their youthful sap, at height decrease,
And wear their brave state out of memory;
Then the conceit of this inconstant stay
Sets you most rich in youth before my sight,   10
Where wasteful time debateth with decay,
To change your day of youth to sulli'd night;
   And all in war with Time for love of you,
   As he takes from you, I engraft you new.

16

To Mr. W. H. urging him to marry.

But wherefore do not you a mightier way
Make war upon this bloody tyrant, time?

And fortify yourself in your decay
With means more blessed than my barren rhyme?
Now stand you on the top of happy hours,   5
And many maidens gardens yet unset
With virtuous wish would bear you living flowers,
Much liker than your painted counterfeit:
So should the lines of life that life repair,
Which this time's pencil, nor my pupil pen,   10
Neither in inward worth nor outward fair,
Can make you live yourself in eyes of men.
  To give away yourself keeps yourself still,
  And you must live, drawn by your own sweet
  skill.

Line 9. Malone quotes with approval the anonymous suggestion that 'the lines of life' means 'living pictures', viz. 'children'.

Line 10, Q. reads 'which this (Times pensell or my pupill pen)'. I adopt Hudson's emendation (Cambridge edition). 'This time's pencil' means 'the pencil of anyone now living', that is to say, 'any living painter'. The sense of the passage is: 'Which neither any living painter, nor my tyro's pen can', etc. Butler rightly claims that the expression 'my pupil pen' is almost conclusive evidence that Shakespeare was very young when he wrote the Sonnets, and that they were the first things he wrote. Is it conceivable that Shakespeare would have referred to his 'pupil pen' after producing those prodigious *tours de force Venus and Adonis* and *Lucrece*? Still less, surely, would he have so described his 'pen' after writing *Love's Labour's Lost*, *The Two Gentlemen of Verona* and *Romeo and Juliet*. Yet nearly all the commentators persist in dating the Sonnets as having been written after these plays, about 1593-4 or later.

One other argument against the supposition that the Sonnets were the first things that Shakespeare wrote may here be dealt with. I mean, of course, that Shakespeare in dedicating his *Venus and Adonis* to Southampton describes it as 'the first heir of my invention'. But it is not disputed that he had already, by the time he had made this dedication, written several plays. It follows that *Venus and Adonis* could not have been strictly speaking, the first heir of his invention. It was, however, his first published work. The Sonnets, as we know, were never published at all till the year 1609, only seven years before his death. At the time when he published *Venus and Adonis*, he probably did not think that the Sonnets would ever be published. He calls *Venus and Adonis* the first heir of his invention simply because it was his first published work.

17

To Mr. W.H. urging him to marry.

Who will believe my verse in time to come,
If it were fill'd with your most high deserts?
Though yet, heav'n knows, it is but as a tomb
Which hides your life and shows not half your parts.
If I could write the beauty of your eyes   5
And in fresh numbers number all your graces,
The age to come would say 'This poet lies;
Such heavenly touches ne'er touch'd earthly faces.'
So should my papers, yellow'd with their age,
Be scorn'd, like old men of less truth than tongue, 10
And your true rights be term'd a Poet's rage
And stretched metre of an antique song:
    But were some child of yours alive that time,
    You should live twice, in it and in my rhyme.

Lines 2 and 4. Note rhymes 'deserts' and 'parts'.
This is the last of the seventeen sonnets in which
Shakespeare urges Mr.W.H. to marry and have children.
I take it that these sonnets cover a space of not more
than a few months. By the time he had got to this
stage it is highly probable that Shakespeare's feelings
had become intensified. His adoration of Mr. W.H.

increased. The pretext of urging him to marry which hitherto had served him as an excuse for extolling the beauty of his friend was worn out. Henceforth, beginning with the lovely sonnet that follows, he dropped that pretext and expressed his feelings quite openly. I have already put on record my conviction that those feelings were perfectly pure and holy.

18

To Mr. W.H. (Here is Thomas Thorpe's 'that eternitie promised by our ever living poet'.)

Shall I compare thee to a summer's day?
Thou art more lovely and more temperate:
Rough winds do shake the darling buds of May
And Summer's lease hath all too short a date:
Sometime too hot the eye of heaven shines,   5
And often is his gold complexion dimm'd;
And every fair from fair sometime declines,
By chance or nature's changing course untrimm'd;
But thy eternal Summer shall not fade
Nor lose possession of that fair thou ow'st;   10
Nor shall death brag thou wander'st in his shade
When in eternal lines to time thou grow'st:
    So long as men can breathe or eyes can see,
    So long lives this;—and this gives life to thee.

19

To Mr. W.H.

Devouring Time, blunt thou the Lion's paws,
And make the earth devour her own sweet brood;
Pluck the keen teeth from the fierce Tiger's jaws,
And burn the long-liv'd Phoenix in her blood;
Make glad and sorry seasons as thou fleet'st, 5
And do whate'er thou wilt, swift-footed Time,
To the wide world and all her fading sweets;
But I forbid thee one most heinous crime:
O, carve not with thy hours my love's fair brow
Nor draw no lines there with thine antique pen; 10
Him in thy course untainted do allow
For beauty's pattern to succeeding men.
 Yet, do thy worst, old Time: despite thy wrong,
 My love shall in my verse ever live young.

20

To Mr. W.H.

A Woman's face with Nature's own hand painted
Hast thou, the Master-Mistress of my passion;
A woman's gentle heart, but not acquainted
With shifting change, as is false women's fashion;
An eye more bright than theirs, less false in rolling, 5

Gilding the object whereupon it gazeth;
A man in hue, all *Hues* in his controlling,
Which steals men's eyes and women's souls amazeth.
And for a woman wert thou first created;
Till nature, as she wrought thee, fell a-doting,   10
And by addition, me of thee defeated
By adding one thing to my purpose nothing.
But since she prick'd thee out for women's pleasure,
Mine be thy love, and thy love's use their treasure.

Line 7. The Quarto reads, 'A man in hew all *Hews* in his controwling.'

Butler acutely points out that the word 'hue' (or 'hew' as the Quarto has it) is here used to mean 'beauty' as in '*O formose puer nimium ne crede colori*'. This is the sonnet which, as first pointed out by Tyrwhitt, endorsed by Malone in 1780, gives the clue to the surname of Mr. W.H. The name Hughes, was indifferently spelt Hughes, Hewes or Hews in Shakespeare's time. Butler has traced a number of persons with the name who were contemporaries of Shakespeare. Wilde, for his part, has discovered ('The Portrait of Mr. W.H.') a musician employed by Lord Pembroke whose name was William Hughes but who was much too old to fill the rôle of Mr. W.H. He suggests that Shakespeare's Will Hughes was perhaps the son of this musician. I have already referred to the fact that Byron in one of his letters refers to 'Master Will Hughes' in a context which shows that Tyrwhitt's and Malone's suggestion was accepted, as a matter of course by Byron and the friend (I think it was Hobhouse) to whom he was writing. As Byron was, like Wilde, a poet, I attach a great deal of importance to his opinion. The opinion of poets, is, in my view, at least as valuable as the opinion of professors or 'eminent Shakespearian scholars' on a question like the one under consideration. Mr. J. M. Robertson airily cuts the sonnet out of the series and says that it was probably written by Barnes! But as he also cuts out and dismisses as 'obviously not by Shakespeare' about fifty others including the sonnets numbered in the Quarto 54, 55 and 56, the first two of which, in my humble opinion (and I also happen to be a poet) are among the finest that Shakespeare has written, I think it is waste of time to argue with him or to take any notice whatever of his fantastic opinions about the Sonnets. The two sonnets to which I refer are: (1) that beginning

'O how much more doth beauty beauteous seem
By that fair ornament which truth doth give!'
and (2) the one beginning
'Not marble nor the gilded monuments
Of princes shall outlive this powerful rhyme!'

Anyone who says that these magnificent sonnets are
'obviously not by Shakespeare' writes himself down
as—well anything that one can say politely! As for
the sonnet last printed (No. 20)

'A woman's face with Nature's own hand painted,'
I should say that it has 'Shakespeare' written all over
it, though it is not one of his finest. As I have already
dealt with it at some length in my preliminary essay
I content myself now with expressing the opinion that
it is really the key sonnet to the whole series. It
expresses Shakespeare's feelings in almost extravagant
terms, it also, as I have already pointed out, proves
that his feelings were perfectly innocent, and, finally,
it furnishes a perfectly plain clue to the surname of
Mr. W.H.

21

To Mr. W.H.

So is it not with me as with that Muse
Stirr'd by a painted beauty to his verse,
Who heav'n itself for ornament doth use
And every fair with his fair doth rehearse,
Making a couplement of proud compare,   5
With sun and moon, with earth and sea's rich gems,

With April's first-born flow'rs, and all things rare
That heaven's air in this huge rondure hems.
Oh, let me, true in love, but truly write,
And then believe me, my love is as fair   10
As any mother's child, though not so bright
As those gold candles fix'd i' the heavens are,
    Let them say more that like of hearsay well;
I will not praise that purpose not to sell.

Line 12, Q. has 'As those gould candells fix't in
heaven's ayer'. The words, 'heaven's ayer', occur only
four lines back. It is hardly likely that Shakespeare
would have used 'heaven's air' twice in five lines. I
therefore adopt Butler's emendation.

22

To Mr. W.H.

My glass shall not persuade me I am old,
So long as youth and thou are of one date;
But when in thee time's furrows I behold
Then look I death my days should expiate.
For all that beauty that doth cover thee   5
Is but the seemly raiment of my heart,
Which in thy breast doth live, as thine in me:
How can I then be elder than thou art?

O, therefore, love, be of thyself so wary
As I, not for myself, but for thee will;   10
Bearing thy heart, which I will keep so chary
As tender nurse her babe from faring ill.
    Presume not on thy heart when mine is slain;
    Thou gav'st me thine, not to give back again.

23

To Mr. W.H.

As an unperfect actor on the stage,
Who with his fear is put besides his part,
Or some fierce thing replete with too much rage,
Whose strength's abundance weakens his own heart;
So I, for fear of trust, forget to say   5
The perfect ceremony of love's rite,
And in mine own love's strength seem to decay,
O'ercharg'd with burthen of mine own love's might.
O, let my looks be then the eloquence
And dumb presagers of my speaking breast;   10
Who plead for love, and look for recompense,
More than that tongue that more hath more ex-
    press'd.
    O, learn to read what silent love hath writ:
    To hear with eyes belongs to love's fine wit.

Line 9, Q. reads: 'O let my books be then', etc.

Malone mentions 'looks' as suggested to him by Capell but rejects it, strangely enough. I adopt it with Butler.

In his comments on this sonnet Butler, in my view, completely goes off the lines of reason and sane deduction. He professes to see in the sonnet the evidence that Shakespeare was in a frame of mind which rendered him an easy victim to the 'luring on' of Mr. W.H. He says 'I find it impossible to believe that the change in Shakespeare's mental attitude evidenced in Sonnet 23 would have been affected unless Mr. W.H. had intended to amuse himself by effecting it. Shakespeare's "looks" would never have become "eloquent", unless he had believed Mr. W.H.'s to have already been so. Mr. W.H. must have lured him on—as we have Shakespeare's word for it that he lured him still more disastrously later. It goes without saying that Shakespeare should not have let himself be lured, but the age was what it was. [Actually it was far less tolerant of what Butler here hints at than the present age is.] And I shall show that Shakespeare was very young.'

All this appears to me to be quite crazy nonsense. Little as I find myself in agreement with Mr. J. M. Robertson, I sympathize with the indignation which this and similar passages in Butler's book have aroused in him. He is very unfair to Butler's patient logic and the enormous amount of trouble he took over the questions of dates and the identity of Mr. W.H. (Butler even learnt all the sonnets by heart and had them, he says, 'at his fingers' ends', before he began to write his book about them.) Mr. Robertson, it seems to me, would have done much better to imitate Butler's industry, and devotion to an incomparable poet, rather than to sneer at him as he does, for wasting time on so many sonnets which Mr. Robertson, with a touching belief in his own infallibility, declares to be obviously spurious. But allowing for all this I do share Mr. Robertson's indignation against what I believe to be the unaccountable stupidity (it is certainly not malice, for he loves Shakespeare) of Butler on this point.

It seems to me that Butler, at this particular point in his investigation, fell into very much the same kind of blunder as the unspeakable Frank Harris (though I would not insult Butler by putting him, generally speaking, in the same category as Harris except in this one respect). That blunder consists in trying to read into Shakespeare's life one's own experiences. Harris has got to the point of saying, and apparently believing, that Shakespeare shared his (Harris's) revolting, almost maniacal, sex-obsession about women. Even Mr. Bernard Shaw shied at this imbecile raving, and for once he dealt faithfully with his friend Harris, leaving him, as was only to be expected, without a leg to stand on or a feather to fly with.

Butler had the misfortune, at one time of his life, to be afflicted with a young friend called Pauli, to whom he was passionately devoted and who treated him in a shocking way; and when he is writing about Shakespeare and Mr. W.H., he is terribly inclined to forget that he is not writing about Butler and Pauli.

He goes on to say 'Between sonnets 32 and 33 Q., I suppose there had been a catastrophe. The trap referred to in the previous paragraph, I believe to have been a cruel and most disgusting practical joke, devised by Mr. W.H. in concert with others, but certainly never intended, much less permitted, to go beyond the raising of coarse laughter against Shakespeare. I cannot doubt that Shakespeare was, to use his words, made to "travel forth" without that "cloak", which, if he had not been lured, he would not have discarded. Hardly had he laid the cloak aside before he was surprised, according to a preconcerted scheme, and very roughly handled, for we find him lame soon afterwards (sonnet 37, lines 3 and 9) and apparently not fully recovered a twelvemonth later (39 Q., line 3).'

I believe all this to be the wildest nonsense. There is not a tittle of evidence to support Butler's story which he never explains or elucidates. I have read his book over and over again to try to find out what he means. What was the 'disgusting practical joke'? He leaves his readers absolutely in the dark; but he founds on this, as I take it, pure figment of his brain, a violent hatred of Mr. W.H. whom he declares to have been a scoundrel and a blackguard, and a heartless wretch who, after seducing Shakespeare into wickedness of a kind not explained but left to be imagined as of a disreputable nature, treated him in a most cruel way and broke his heart.

Butler has no warrant for any such inferences. As one reads his book one keeps on supposing that he is going to explain exactly what he means and make good his preposterous story. But he does nothing of the kind. I believe he simply transposed his own experiences into the story of Shakespeare, very much as Harris did.

I do not believe that when Shakespeare speaks of going out 'without his cloak', he is referring to an actual material cloak; nor do I think that his references to the 'lameness' should be taken literally. But even if they were so to be taken, they afford no grounds at all, for Butler's absurd conclusions, or for his violent abuse of Mr. W.H. That Shakespeare ultimately quarrelled with the latter we may believe or not. But even if he did, which I doubt, what right have we to assume that the fault was all on the side of Mr. W.H.?, 'Devouring Time', in spite of Shakespeare's protests, no doubt dealt with Mr. W.H. in the usual way. Perhaps, after all, the greatest sin in Shakespeare's eyes of which he was guilty was that he lost his looks.

Moreover, according to Butler's own showing, Shakespeare went on adoring him for two years after the 'disgusting practical joke', and when (according to Butler's version) he did ultimately quarrel with him the worst he called him was a 'suborned informer'.

Butler, as so often happens in the case of would-be 'defenders' of an injured man, really does Shakespeare the worst possible service. He invents his wonderful story about the 'practical joke', and after leaving the matter in a complete fog of hints and ambiguity, he proceeds to come out quite roundly with an accusation of homosexuality against Shakespeare. This is what he says:

'The offence above indicated, a sin of very early youth, for which Shakespeare was bitterly penitent, and towards which not a trace of further tendency

74

can be discerned in any subsequent sonnet or work during five-and-twenty years of prolific literary activities—this single offence is the utmost that can be brought against Shakespeare with a shadow of evidence in its support.'

All I can say is that if Butler had written such a libel on a living man on the strength of similar 'evidence', he would have been lucky to have escaped criminal prosecution.

But what I would like to put to my readers is the question whether 'eminent Shakespearian scholars' do not do Shakespeare just as great an injury by refusing to accept the plain meaning of the Sonnets, illuminated as they are by the dedication of Thomas Thorpe, and by treating the whole matter as a thing which must be either totally ignored, or explained away by the most idiotic and transparent attempts to throw dust into the eyes of enquirers.

On the one hand we have commentators like Sir Sydney Lee who have the face to suggest seriously that a sonnet beginning with the words

'A woman's face with Nature's own hand painted,
Hast thou the Master-Mistress of my passion.'

was merely a complimentary address to a noble literary

patron in the person of Pembroke or Southampton (Lee declared first that Pembroke was obviously the addressee, and some time later he declared with equal confidence that it must be Southampton).

On the other hand we have critics like Hallam who say that 'it is impossible not to wish that Shakespeare had never written' the Sonnets. Any indignation one feels against Butler (who at least was honest) must be equally felt against the type of 'Shakespearian Scholar' represented by Hallam. These two 'schools of thought' (the Lee school and the Hallam school) cover almost the entire field of commentators, who one and all seem to lose their heads and their common sense when they come to deal with the Sonnets as distinct from the plays.

24

To Mr. W.H.

Mine eye hath play'd the painter, and hath steel'd
Thy beauty's form in table of my heart;
My body is the frame wherein 'tis held,
And perspective it is best Painter's art.
For through the Painter must you see his skill, 5
To find where your true Image pictur'd lies;
Which in my bosom's shop is hanging still,

That hath his windows glazed with thine eyes.
Now see what good turns eyes for eyes have done:
Mine eyes have drawn thy shape, and thine for me   10
Are windows to my breast where-through the Sun
Delights to peep, to gaze therein on thee;
    Yet eyes this cunning want to grace their art,
    They draw but what they see, know not the heart.

Line 4, 'perspective' must be pronounced with
accent on the first syllable thus: 'pèrspective'.

25

To Mr. W.H.

Let those who are in favour with their stars
Of public honour and proud titles boast,
Whilst I, whom fortune of such triumph bars,
Unlook'd for joy in that I honour most.
Great Princes' favourites their fair leaves spread   5
But as the Marigold at the sun's eye,
And in themselves their pride lies buried,
For at a frown they in their glory die.
The painful warrior famoused for fight,
After a thousand victories once foil'd,   10
Is from the book of honour razed quite,
And all the rest forgot for which he toil'd;

Then happy I, that love and am belov'd
Where I may not remove, nor be remov'd.

Line 9, Q. reads 'famosed for worth' which does not
not rhyme. I adopt Theobald's emendation endorsed
by Malone.

This sonnet is in my opinion absolutely conclusive
evidence, against the Pembroke or Southampton
theories. Shakespeare is contrasting his own as yet
humble and unhonoured position with that of more
fortunate persons who are the favourites of great
princes. How could he do this if he were, in fact, at
the time he wrote the sonnet, a favoured client of great
nobles like Pembroke or Southampton? Again, how
could he say, if he were the *protégé* of Pembroke or
Southampton, that he 'may not be removed', whereas
evidently he may be 'removed' at any time out of the
favour of either of these noblemen?

26

To Mr. W.H.

Lord of my love, to whom in vassalage,
Thy merit hath my duty strongly knit,
To thee I send this written ambassage,
To witness duty, not to show my wit:

Duty so great, which wit so poor as mine   5
May make seem bare, in wanting words to show it,
But that I hope some good conceit of thine
In thy soul's thought, all naked, will bestow it;
Till whatsoever star that guides my moving,
Points on me graciously with fair aspect,   10
And puts apparel on my tatter'd loving,
To show me worthy of thy sweet respect:
 Then may I dare to boast how I do love thee;
 Till then not show my head where thou mayst
 prove me.

Line 10, 'aspect' pronounced 'aspèct'. (Conf. 'The sweet aspèct of princes', *Henry VIII*, iii, 2.)

This sonnet is certainly much more like a complimentary address to a great nobleman. If it stood alone it might be so accepted, but its place in the series and context, make such an assumption impossible. Butler suggests that it was possibly sent to Mr. W.H. by Shakespeare in a letter containing the six next following sonnets.

27

To Mr. W.H.

Weary with toil, I haste me to my bed,
The dear repose for limbs with travail tir'd;

79

But then begins a journey in my head,
To work my mind, when body's work's expir'd:
For then my thoughts, from far where I abide,   5
Intend a zealous pilgrimage to thee,
And keep my drooping eyelids open wide,
Looking on darkness which the blind do see:
Save that my soul's imaginary sight
Presents thy shadow to my sightless view,   10
Which, like a jewel hung in ghastly night,
Makes black night beauteous and her old face new,
  Lo, thus, by day my limbs, by night my mind,
  For thee and for myself no quiet find.

Line 11, conf. *Romeo and Juliet* i, 5.
'It seems she hangs upon the cheek of night,
Like a rich jewel in an Ethiope's ear.'

28

To Mr. W.H.

How can I, then, return in happy plight,
That am debarr'd the benefit of rest?
When day's oppression is not eas'd by night,
But day by night, and night by day, oppress'd?
And each, though enemies to either's reign,   5

Do in consent shakes hands to torture me;
The one by toil, the other to complain
How far I toil, still farther off from thee.
I tell the Day, to please him, thou art bright,
And dost him grace when clouds do blot the heaven: 10
So flatter I the swart-complexion'd Night;
When sparkling stars twire not, thou gild'st the even.
   But day doth daily draw my sorrows longer,
   And night doth nightly make grief's length seem
     stronger.

Lines 9-12. The sense is 'I tell the day that even when there are clouds in the sky you are there to grace him, and so with night when there are no stars.'

29

To Mr. W.H.

When, in disgrace with Fortune and men's eyes,
I all alone beweep my outcast state,
Trouble deaf heaven with my bootless cries,
And look upon myself, and curse my fate,
Wishing me like to one more rich in hope,   5
Featur'd like him, like him with friends possess'd,
Desiring this man's art and that man's scope,
With what I most enjoy contented least;

Yet in these thoughts myself almost despising,
Haply I think on thee, and then my state,   10
Like to the Lark at break of day arising
From sullen earth, sings hymns at Heaven's gate;
   For thy sweet love remember'd such wealth brings
   That then I scorn to change my state with kings.

Line 3. Following the Quarto this line is invariably printed: 'And trouble deaf heaven with my bootless cries.'

I have ventured to cut out the 'And' to make the line scan. The line as generally printed is a syllable too long, and the sense does not require the 'and' which was probably a printer's error from the 'and' which begins the next line.

This sonnet again is a strong argument against the Pembroke or Southampton theories. How could Shakespeare describe himself, in a sonnet addressed to either of these powerful and wealthy patrons, as being outcast, hopeless and friendless?

The plain sense of the sonnet is: 'I am miserable, poor, unfriended and unhonoured, but in the depths of my wretchedness I have the supreme consolation of knowing that I love you and that you love me in return.'

30

To Mr. W.H.

When to the sessions of sweet silent thought
I summon up remembrance of things past,
I sigh the lack of many a thing I sought,
And with old woes new wail my dear times' waste:
Then can I drown an eye unus'd to flow,   5
For precious friends hid in death's dateless night,
And weep afresh love's long-since cancell'd woe,
And moan the expense of many a vanish'd sight.
Then can I grieve at grievances foregone,
And heavily from woe to woe tell o'er   10
The sad account of fore-bemoaned moan,
Which I new pay as if not paid before,
    But if the while I think on thee, dear friend,
    All losses are restor'd, and sorrows end.

Line 8. Malone declares that 'sight' here means 'sigh'.

31

To Mr. W.H.

Thy bosom is endeared with all hearts,
Which I by lacking have supposed dead;

And there reigns Love and all Love's loving parts,
And all those friends which I thought buried.
How many a holy and obsequious tear   5
Hath dear religious love stol'n from mine eye,
As interest of the dead, which now appear
But things remov'd, that hidden in thee lie!
Thou art the grave where buri'd love doth live,
Hung with the trophies of my lovers gone,   10
Who all their parts of me to thee did give,
That due of many now is thine alone:
    Their images I lov'd I view in thee,
    And thou (all they) hast all the all of me.

Line 8, Q. reads, 'hidden in there lie'. The emendation is by Gildon, given in the Cambridge edition.

32

To Mr. W.H.

If thou survive my well-contented day,
When that churl death my bones with dust shall
    cover,
And shalt by fortune once more re-survey
These poor rude lines of thy deceased Lover,
Compare them with the bett'ring of the time,   5
And though they be outstripp'd by every pen,

Reserve them for my love, not for their rhyme,
Exceeded by the height of happier men.
O, then vouchsafe me but this loving thought:
'Had my friend's Muse grown with his growing age,
A dearer birth than this his love had brought,   11
To march in ranks of better equipage:
  But since he died, and Poets better prove,
  Theirs for their style I'll read, his for his love.'

Line 10, Q. reads: 'Had my friends Muse growne with this growing age.'

Hudson's emendation 'his' for 'this', which the sense obviously demands, is here adopted.

Butler has a note at the foot of this sonnet as follows: 'Between the writing of this sonnet and the next (121 Q.) there had been a catastrophe. For the nature of this, and for the reasons which have led me to place 121 Q. here, see Chapter 9.' Sonnet 121 in the Quarto is the one beginning:

' 'Tis better to be vile than vile esteemed,'

and Butler placing it next after the sonnet printed on this page has a sub-heading: 'To Mr. W.H. Written by Shakespeare before he had calmed down after the catastrophe referred to in the preceding note'. I agree with Butler that this sonnet is wrongly placed in the Quarto. I cannot, indeed I would have no right, to reproduce here the arguments which he uses, because it would entail quoting a whole chapter out of his book, which ought to be read by every student of the Sonnets. I accept his emendations of the order in which the sonnets should appear, except in the cases already referred to of the poem (not a sonnet) which I have already placed before the Sonnets and the sonnet beginning 'The expense of Spirit in a waste of Shame' which he takes altogether out of the series, but which I believe to refer to the 'dark woman'.

As to what Butler calls the 'catastrophe', I agree that obviously something of a painful nature had occurred which resulted in a quarrel. But I can see no support at all for Butler's suggested 'disgusting, practical joke', or the 'trap' into which he says Shakespeare fell.

33 (121 Q.)

To Mr. W.H.

'Tis better to be vile than vile esteemed,
When not to be, receives reproach of being;
And the just pleasure lost, which is so deem'd
Not by our feeling, but by others' seeing:
For why should others' false adulterate eyes   5
Give salutation to my sportive blood?
Or on my frailties why are frailer spies,

Which in their wills count bad what I think good?
No, I am that I am; and they that level
At my abuses, reckon up their own: 10
I may be straight, though they themselves be bevel;
By their rank thoughts my deeds must not be shown;
   Unless this general evil they maintain,—
   All men are bad, and in their badness reign.

This sonnet is very obscure. I agree with Butler
that it belongs to the group we have now reached in
the Sonnets. If it is kept where the Quarto puts it,
it 'makes hay' of the continuity of the story. It fits in
here as being the first sonnet written after a quarrel, or
disagreeable episode of some sort which overshadows
the four following sonnets.

Its sense appears to be: 'I have been abused and
calumniated, whereas I have done nothing wrong or
of which I am ashamed. People who condemn me do
so out of the rank badness of their own minds.'
Evidently Shakespeare is angry and hurt, but his anger
does not seem to be directed against Mr. W.H. as
Butler would appear to imply.

Putting it in conjunction with the sonnet which comes
third in order after it, 'Let me confess that we two must
be twain,' I conjecture that it refers to some evil
speaking about Shakespeare's friendship for Mr. W.H.

34 (33 Q.)

To Mr. W.H.

Full many a glorious morning have I seen
Flatter the mountain-tops with sovereign eye,
Kissing with golden face the meadows green,
Gilding pale streams with heavenly alchemy;
Anon permit the basest clouds to ride   5
With ugly rack on his celestial face,
And from the forlorn world his visage hide,
Stealing unseen to west with his disgrace:
Even so my Sun one early morn did shine
With all-triumphant splendour on my brow;   10
But, out, alack! he was but one hour mine,
The region cloud hath mask'd him from me now.
    Yet him for this my love no whit disdaineth;
    Suns of the world may stain when heaven's sun
        staineth.

Line 8, Q. reads: 'With this disgrace' the emendation to 'his' is Hudson's.

Shakespeare here complains, in a very mild, affectionate and forgiving way. Is this the sort of sonnet which the victim of a 'disgusting practical joke' would write? I trow not.

35 (34 Q.)

To Mr. W.H.

Why didst thou promise such a beauteous day
And make me travel forth without my cloak,
To let base clouds o'ertake me in my way,
Hiding thy brav'ry in their rotten smoke?
'Tis not enough that through the cloud thou break   5
To dry the rain on my storm-beaten face,
For no man well of such a salve can speak
That heals the wound, and cures not the disgrace:
Nor can thy shame give physic to my grief;
Though thou repent, yet I have still the loss: 10
The offender's sorrow lends but weak relief
To him that bears the strong offence's cross.
   Ah! but those tears are pearl which thy love sheds,
   And they are rich, and ransom all ill deeds.

Line 2. 'And make me travel forth without my cloak.' In contradiction to Butler I take this to be purely figurative.

36

To Mr. W.H.

Let me confess that we two must be twain,
Although our undivided loves are one:

So shall those blots that do with me remain,
Without thy help, by me be borne alone.
In our two loves there is but one respect,   5
Though in our lives a separable spite,
Which though it alter not love's sole effect,
Yet doth it steal sweet hours from love's delight.
I may not evermore acknowledge thee,
Lest my bewailed guilt should do thee shame,   10
Nor thou with public kindness honour me,
Unless thou take that honour from thy name:
   But do not so; I love thee in such sort,
   As thou being mine, mine is thy good report.

Line 10. Butler heads this sonnet 'a sequel to the
preceding sonnet'. It is so, but it is in strange contradiction with it. Whereas in the preceding sonnet
Shakespeare appears to blame and reproach his friend,
and to say that even his repentance for the wrong he
has done cannot altogether make up for the 'strong
offence's cross', he now speaks of his own 'bewailed
guilt' and tells Mr. W.H. that he cannot honour him
(Shakespeare) with 'public kindness' without incurring
loss of honour to his (Mr. W.H.'s) name. I think all
this completely disposes of Butler's theory that Mr.
W.H. had been guilty of some blackguardly conduct.
If we are to accept what Shakespeare says when he

blames his friend, why are we to take less notice when
he blames himself and admits 'guilt'?

37

To Mr. W.H.

As a decrepit father takes delight
To see his active child do deeds of youth,
So I, made lame by Fortune's dearest spite,
Take all my comforts of thy worth and truth;
For whether beauty, birth, or wealth, or wit,   5
Or any of these all, or all, or more,
Entitled in thy parts do crowned sit,
I make my love engrafted to this store:
So then I am not lame, poor, nor despis'd,
Whilst that this shadow doth such substance give 10
That I in thy abundance am suffic'd
And by a part of all thy glory live.
    Look, what is best, that best I wish in thee:
    This wish I have; then ten times happy me!

Line 3. Malone maintains that the 'lameness' in this
line and in line 9 is metaphorical. I agree with him.
Butler insists that it is to be taken literally in that
Shakespeare's lameness was the result of the 'disgusting practical joke' which is the bee in his (Butler's)
bonnet.

38

To Mr. W.H.

How can my Muse want subject to invent,
While thou dost breathe, that pour'st into my verse
Thine own sweet argument, too excellent
For every vulgar paper to rehearse?
O, give thyself the thanks, if aught in me   5
Worthy perusal stand against thy sight:
For who's so dumb that cannot write to thee,
When thou thyself dost give invention light?
Be thou the tenth Muse, ten times more in worth
Than those old nine, which rhymers invocate;   10
And he that calls on thee, let him bring forth
Eternal numbers to outlive long date.
    If my slight Muse do please these curious days,
    The pain be mine, but thine shall be the praise.

39

To Mr. W.H.

O, how thy worth with manners may I sing,
When thou art all the better part of me?
What can mine own praise to mine own self bring?
And what is't but mine own when I praise thee?

Even for this let us divided live,   5
And our dear love lose name of single one,
That by this separation I may give
That due to thee which thou deserv'st alone.
O absence, what a torment wouldst thou prove,
Were it not thy sour leisure gave sweet leave   10
To entertain the time with thoughts of love,
Which time and thoughts so sweetly doth deceive,
   And that thou teachest how to make one twain,
   By praising him here who doth hence remain!

40 (127 Q.)

Concerning Shakespeare's Mistress.

In the old age black was not counted fair,
Or if it were, it bore not beauty's name;
But now is black beauty's successive heir,
And beauty slander'd with a bastard shame:
For since each hand hath put on nature's power   5
Fairing the foul with art's false borrow'd face,
Sweet beauty hath no name, no holy bower,
But is profan'd, if not lives in disgrace.
Therefore my mistress' eyes are raven black,
Her eyes so suited, and they mourners seem   10
At such who, not born fair, no beauty lack,
Sland'ring creation with a false esteem:

Yet so they mourn, becoming of their woe,
That every tongue says beauty should look so.

This sonnet (numbered 127 in the Quarto) which
Butler puts here for convincing reasons which are
given at length in his book, begins the 'Dark Woman'
series. Observe at once the difference in tone from the
adoring sonnets to Mr. W.H. Shakespeare, as I take
it, had a short, entirely physical infatuation for this
woman, but he seldom finds himself able to write
about her without showing plainly enough that he
despised and disliked her. There is no evidence worth
writing about to identify her with Mary Fitton. The
fact that Frank Harris was convinced that she was
Mary Fitton is enough in itself to make one feel pretty
sure that she was not. Harris is not only 'certain' that
the 'dark woman' was Mary Fitton, but he concludes
that Shakespeare remained under her thrall for the
greater part of his life and that she appears in most of
his plays! This is so patently ridiculous that it is not
worth refuting.

41 (128 Q.)

To Shakespeare's Mistress.

How oft, when thou, my music, music play'st,
Upon that blessed wood whose motion sounds

With thy sweet fingers, when thou gently sway'st
The wiry concord that mine ear confounds,
Do I envy those jacks that nimble leap   5
To kiss the tender inward of thy hand,
Whilst my poor lips which should that harvest reap,
At the wood's boldness by thee blushing stand!
To be so tickled, they would change their state
And situation with those dancing chips,   10
O'er whom thy fingers walk with gentle gait,
Making dead wood more bless'd than living lips.
  Since saucy jacks so happy are in this,
  Give them thy fingers, me thy lips to kiss.

Line 5, 'envy' pronounced 'envỳ'.

42 (129 Q.)

Expressing Shakespeare's feelings about his mistress,
and epitomizing his life-long attitude towards any
kind of sexual intercourse outside marriage.

The expense of Spirit in a waste of shame
Is lust in action; and till action, lust
Is perjur'd, murd'rous, bloody, full of blame,
Savage, extreme, rude, cruel, not to trust;
Enjoy'd no sooner but despised straight;   5

Past reason hunted; and no sooner had,
Past reason hated, as a swallow'd bait,
On purpose laid to make the taker mad:
Mad in pursuit, and in possession so;
Had, having, and in quest to have, extreme;   10
A bliss in proof, and prov'd, a very woe;
Before, a joy propos'd; behind, a dream.
 All this the world well knows; yet none knows well
 To shun the heaven that leads men to this hell.

Butler, as I have already said, puts this sonnet by itself as an 'occasional sonnet probably given, but not addressed to Mr. W.H., nor in any way referring to him'. I, on the other hand, leave it in its place in the Quarto in relation to the 'Dark Woman' series (of which it is the third) beginning with 127 Q. and ending with 152 Q.

When I say in the sub-heading which I have affixed to this sonnet that it epitomizes Shakespeare's lifelong attitude towards illicit 'love'[1], I am not claiming that Shakespeare (who was unhappily married) led an enturely virtuous life. For all I know he may have had

---

[1] 'call it not love, for Love to heaven has fled
Since sweating lust on earth usurp'd his name.'
  Shakespeare—*Venus and Adonis*.

dozens of other mistresses, though I think it exceedingly improbable. But the evidence of his attitude all through his plays towards the whole question of license and chastity is overwhelmingly on the side of chastity. But why argue about it? I refer opponents back to this tremendous sonnet which is the fiercest attack on the 'facts of life' school, represented by persons like H. G. Wells, the late Arnold Bennett and Frank Harris, which has ever been put into words. I could quote a hundred parallel passages from the plays.

43 (130 Q.)

Concerning Shakespeare's Mistress
(a very insulting sonnet)

My Mistress' eyes are nothing like the sun;
Coral is far more red than her lips' red:
If snow be white, why then her breasts are dun;
If hairs be wire, black wires grow on her head.
I have seen roses damask'd, red and white,   5
But no such roses see I in her cheeks;
And in some perfumes is there more delight
That in the breath that from my Mistress reeks.
I love to hear her speak—yet well I know
That music hath a far more pleasing sound: 10

I grant I never saw a goddess go.
My Mistress, when she walks, treads on the ground.
    And yet, by heaven, I think my love as rare
    As any she belied with false compare.

44 (131 Q.)

To Shakespeare's Mistress.

Thou art as tyrannous, so as thou art,
As those whose beauties proudly make them cruel;
For well thou know'st to my dear doting heart
Thou art the fairest and most precious jewel.
Yet, in good faith, some say that thee behold,   5
Thy face hath not the power to make love groan:
To say they err, I dare not be so bold,
Although I swear it to myself alone.
And, to be sure that is not false I swear,
A thousand groans, but thinking on thy face,   10
One on another's neck, do witness bear
Thy black is fairest in my judgment's place.
    In nothing art thou black, save in thy deeds,
    And thence this slander, as I think proceeds.

Observe the ferocity of the last two lines coming to
finish this commonplace and uninspired sonnet.

45 (132 Q.)

To Shakespeare's Mistress.

Thine eyes I love, and they, as pitying me,
Knowing thy heart torments me with disdain,
Have put on black, and loving mourners be,
Looking with pretty ruth upon my pain.
And truly not the morning Sun of Heaven   5
Better becomes the grey cheeks of the East,
Nor that full Star that ushers in the Even,
Doth half that glory to the sober West,
As those two mourning eyes become thy face:
O, let it, then, as well beseem thy heart   10
To mourn for me, since mourning doth thee grace,
And suit thy pity 'like in every part.
 Then will I swear beauty herself is black,
 And all they foul that thy complexion lack.

46 (137 Q.)

To Shakespeare's Mistress
(More insults)

Thou blind fool, love, what dost thou to mine eyes,
That they behold, and see not what they see?
They know what beauty is, see where it lies,

Yet what the best is take the worst to be.
If eyes, corrupt by over-partial looks,   5
Be anchor'd in the bay where all men ride,
Why of eyes, falsehood hast thou forged hooks,
Whereto the judgement of my heart is ti'd?
Why should my heart think that a several plot
Which my heart knows the wide world's common
    place?   10
Or mine eyes seeing this, say this is not,
To put fair truth upon so foul a face?
  In things right true my heart and eyes have err'd,
  And to this false plague are they now transferr'd.

47 (138 Q.)

Concerning Shakespeare's Mistress
(Not at all complimentary)

When my love swears that she is made of truth,
I do believe her, though I know she lies,
That she might think me some untutor'd youth,
Unlearned in the world's false subleties.
Thus vainly thinking that she thinks me young,   5
Although she knows my days are past the best,
Simply I credit her false-speaking tongue:
On both sides thus is simple truth supprest.

But wherefore says she not she is unjust?
And wherefore say not I that am old?   10
O, love's best habit is in seeming trust,
And age in love loves not to have years told:
   Therefore I lie with her, and she with me,
   And in our faults by lies we flatter'd be.

Lines 5, 6 and 10 in this poor sonnet raise the
question of Shakespeare's age when he wrote this and
the rest of the Sonnets. According to Butler's reckoning, the strength of which I shall refer to later on in its
due place, Shakespeare was about twenty-one and a
half when he wrote this sonnet, and twenty-four and a
half, roughly, when he wrote the last of the Sonnets
(125 Q.). Yet he here calls himself 'past the best' and
'old'. But Butler points out that what Shakespeare
then called 'old' was probably what we should call
very young. We have already seen from sonnets 2 and
3 that Shakespeare looked upon a man of forty (or
even thirty-seven in sonnet 3) as completely worn out
with one foot in the grave and 'deep-sunken eyes'.
Shakespeare was at least three or four years older than
Mr. W.H. and at that age, twenty-one to twenty-four,
young men are very inclined to think themselves 'old'
even in the present day. I have heard undergraduates of
nineteen or twenty, in this year of grace at Oxford,

talk quite gravely about 'when I was young'; and I find an amusing instance of the same phenomenon in my own case. The first serious poem I ever wrote, which appeared in the *Oxford Magazine* when I was in my second year at Magdalen and about nineteen years old, is called 'Autumn Days'. Anyone reading it, without knowing anything about its date, would put down the author's age as at least sixty. It is all about death and decay and ruined hopes, although at the time I wrote it I was a supremely healthy and athletic youth, devoted to sport of all kinds, and a long distance runner! It has this stanza:

> And the bracken was like yellow gold
> That comes too late,
> When the heart is sad and old,
> And death at the gate,

I can also remember that when I celebrated my twenty-first birthday at Oxford, at a dinner given in my honour by the late Lord Encombe who shared rooms with me in 'the High', I was so overcome with melancholy at the thought of my 'vanished youth' that I retired after dinner to my bedroom and wept.

Butler is very good on this point and I would like to quote him in full, but I prefer to send readers to his own book. I quote, shortly only, as follows, with reference to the sonnet we are now considering, 47 (138 Q.):

'Hence . . . we may infer that "old" which it seems from the same sonnet, only means "past the best" may intend nothing more than "past the fluffy stage". Sonnet 22 does indeed show that Shakespeare was older than Mr. W.H., but a difference of three or four years would be enough to make him seem old by comparison both to himself and to his friend, especially when we remember that he had married imprudently at eighteen . . . moreover, even the Southamptonites ought not to make Shakespeare older than, say, twenty-eight, when sonnet 22 was written, and if at this age he could persuade himself into thinking that his glass ought to persuade him he was old, he could so persuade himself at twenty-one. Besides, he repeatedly abases his own appearance by comparison with that of his friend. Seeing, then, how impossible it is that Shakespeare should have been really old, or even elderly, when he wrote sonnet 22, his implying that he was then old points rather in the direction of thinking that he was young.'

Butler also quotes Malone, when, referring to sonnet 32, line 10:

'Had my friend's Muse grown with his growing age,' he writes: 'We may hence, as well as from other circumstances, infer that these (i.e., the Sonnets) were among our author's earliest compositions.'

48 (139 Q.)

To Shakespeare's Mistress, who is now making up to someone else, presumably Mr. W.H.

O, call me not to justify the wrong
That thy unkindness lays upon my heart;
Wound me not with thine eye, but with thy tongue;
Use pow'r with pow'r, and slay me not by Art.
Tell me thou lov'st elsewhere; but in my sight,   5
Dear heart, forbear to glance thine eye aside:
What need'st thou wound with cunning, when thy
    might
Is more than my o'erpress'd defence can 'bide?
Let me excuse thee: ah my love well knows
Her pretty looks have been my enemies;   10
And therefore from my face she turns my foes,
That they elsewhere might dart their injuries:
    Yet do not so; but since I am near slain,
    Kill me outright with looks, and rid my pain.

49 (140 Q.)

To Shakespeare's Mistress

Be wise as thou art cruel: do not press
My tongue-tied patience with too much disdain;
Lest sorrow lend me words, and words express
The manner of my pity-wanting pain.
If I might teach thee wit, better it were,   5
Though not to love, yet, love, to tell me so;
As testy sick men, when their deaths be near,
No news but health from their Physicians know;
For, if I should despair, I should grow mad,
And in my madness might speak ill of thee: 10
Now this ill-wresting world is grown so bad,
Mad sland'rers by mad ears believed be.
    That I may not be so, nor thou beli'd,
      Bear thine eyes straight, though thy proud heart
        go wide.

50 (141 Q.)

To Shakespeare's Mistress

In faith, I do not love thee with mine eyes,
For they in thee a thousand errors note;
But 'tis my heart that loves what they despise,
Who, in despite of view, is pleas'd to dote;
Nor are mine ears with thy tongue's tune delighted; 5

Nor tender feeling to base touch is prone,
Nor taste, nor smell, desire to be invited
To any sensual feast with thee alone:
But my five wits nor my five senses can
Dissuade one foolish heart from serving thee,   10
Who leaves unsway'd the likeness of a man,
Thy proud heart's slave and vassal wretch to be:
   Only my plague thus far I count my gain,
   That she that makes me sin awards me pain.

Line 6, Q. has 'Nor tender feeling to base touches prone'.

I adopt Butler's emendation.

This bitter and insulting sonnet shows once more that Shakespeare was enthralled to his mistress only by the senses and against his better self.

Lines 13 and 14. I take this to be a very Catholic sentiment. It means: 'The only consolation I can get out of my sin is that while you make me sin, you also make me suffer, thus anticipating my Purgatory.'

51 (142 Q.)

To Shakespeare's Mistress

Love is my sin and thy dear virtue hate,
Hate of my sin, grounded on sinful loving;
O, but with mine compare thou thine own state,

And thou shalt find it merits not reproving;
Or, if it do, not from those lips of thine,   5
That have profan'd their scarlet ornaments
And seal'd false bonds of love as oft as mine,
Robb'd others' beds' revenues of their rents.
Be't lawful I love thee, as thou lov'st those
Whom thine eyes woo as mine importune thee;   10
Root pity in thy heart, that when it grows
Thy pity may deserve to piti'd be.
　　If thou dost seek to have what thou dost hide,
　　By self-example mayst thou be denied!

Line 8. 'Revenues' pronounced 'revènues' as in Shakespeare *passim*.

Line 12. Considering the ugly split infinitive in this line, I almost envy Mr. J. M. Robertson's lighthearted propensity to dismiss as 'obviously spurious' any sonnet that does not appeal to him or fit in with his theories. With one exception, in *Julius Caesar*, it is the only split infinitive to be found in the whole enormous mass of Shakespeare's writing. It is appropriate that it should occur in one of his worst sonnets, which, to my mind is redeemed by only one fine line, precisely the line that Mr. Robertson singles out to support his attack on the genuineness of the sonnet, I mean line 6:
'That have profan'd their scarlet ornaments.'

52 (143 Q.)

To Shakespeare's mistress who is now in full pursuit of a reluctant youth named Will—Mr. W.H. to wit.

Lo, as a careful housewife runs to catch
One of her feather'd creatures broke away,
Sets down her babe, and makes all swift dispatch
In pursuit of the thing she would have stay;
Whilst her neglected child holds her in chase,   5
Cries to catch her whose busy care is bent
To follow that which flies before her face,
Not prizing her poor infant's discontent:
So runn'st thou after that which flies from thee,
Whilst I thy babe chase thee afar behind;   10
But if thou catch thy hope, turn back to me,
And play the mother's part, kiss me, be kind:
    So will I pray that thou mayst have thy *Will*,
    If thou turn back and my loud crying still.

Line 4, 'pursuit' pronounced 'pùrsuit'.
Lines 13-14. '*Will*' here obviously means Mr. W.H., and Shakespeare says in effect: 'provided you do not abandon me altogether I am quite content to let you have him'.

53 (144 Q.)

Concerning Mr. W.H. and Shakespeare's mistress.

Two loves I have of comfort and despair.
Which like two spirits do suggest me still:
The better angel is a man right fair,
The worser spirit a woman colour'd ill.
To win me soon to hell, my female evil   5
Tempteth my better angel from my side,
And would corrupt my saint to be a devil,
Wooing his purity with her foul pride.
And whether that my angel be turn'd fiend
Suspect I may, yet not directly tell;   10
But being both from me, both to each friend,
I guess one angel in another's hell:
     Yet this shall I ne'er know, but live in doubt,
     Till my bad angel fire my good one out.

Lines 2 and 4. The word 'spirit' is two syllables in
the first line and one syllable in the fourth.

My comments on this most important sonnet, which
is one of the key sonnets to the whole series, appear on
pages 27, 28 and 29.

54 (135 Q.)

To Shakespeare's Mistress.
Probably written by Shakespeare for Mr. W.H. to
give to his (Shakespeare's) mistress as though written
by himself.

Whoever hath her wish, thou hast thy *Will*
And *Will* to boot, and *Will* in overplus;
More than enough am I that vex thee still,
To thy sweet will making addition thus.
Wilt thou, whose will is large and spacious,   5
Not once vouchsafe to hide my will in thine?
Shall will in others seem right gracious,
And in my will no fair acceptance shine?
The sea, all water, yet receives rain still,
And in abundance addeth to his store;   10
So thou, being rich in *Will*, add to thy *Will*
One will of mine, to make thy large *Will* more.
    Let no unkindness fair beseechers kill;
    Think all but one, and me in that one *Will*.

Line 1. The *Will* here means Shakespeare.
Line 2. Both the *Wills* here are Mr. W.H.
Lines 11 and 12. All three *Wills* here are Shakespeare.

Line 14. *Will* here is Mr. W.H.

Line 13, Q. reads 'Let no unkinde, no faire beseechers kill'.

I take Butler's emendation.

This sonnet, to my mind, can only be explained by supposing that Shakespeare wrote it for Mr. W.H. to give to his (Shakespeare's) mistress as if written by Mr. W.H. himself. This interpretation implies that Mr. W.H., who evidently at first had resisted the advances of the 'dark woman', had now changed his mind, and anxious to make up for his former coldness and disdain, now wished to get into her good graces. She was by this time probably offended at Mr. W.H.'s rejection of her advances, or at any rate pretended to be offended. She drew off to draw him on, with evident success. Shakespeare, who really cared nothing for his mistress, as we have seen quite plainly from the insulting way he writes about her, at Mr. W.H.'s request, wrote this sonnet for him.

I do not like this interpretation, but it is forced upon me.

The only alternative suggestion I can offer is that Mr. W.H. wrote this sonnet and the next himself. They are both very inferior sonnets nor worthy of a great poet, and if we could believe that Mr. W.H. wrote them himself it would relieve Shakespeare of a

somewhat unpleasant rôle. But I offer this suggestion
with no confidence.

55 (136 Q.)

Written by Shakespeare for Mr. W.H. to give to his
(Shakespeare's) mistress, as though written by himself.

If thy soul check thee that I come so near,
Swear to thy blind soul that I was thy *Will*,
And will, thy soul knows, is admitted there;
Thus far for love, my love-suit, sweet, fulfil.
Will will fulfil the treasure of thy love,   5
Ay, fill it full with wills, and my will one.
In things of great receipt with ease we prove,
Among a number one is reckon'd none;
Then in the number let me pass untold,
Though in thy stores' account I one must be;   10
For nothing hold me, so it please thee hold
That nothing me, a something sweet to thee:
   Make but my name thy love, and love that still,
   And then thou lov'st me—for my name is *Will*.

Line 2. *Will* here is Shakespeare.
Line 5. *Will* here is Shakespeare.

Line 6, Q. reads: 'I fill it full with wils'.
I adopt Malone's emendation.

Line 14. *Will* here is Mr. W.H.

56 (151 Q.)

To Shakespeare's Mistress.

Love is too young to know what conscience is;
Yet who knows not, conscience is born of love?
Then, gentle cheater, urge not my amiss,
Lest guilty of my faults thy sweet self prove;
For, thou betraying me, I do betray   5
My nobler part to my gross body's treason:
My soul doth tell my body that he may
Triumph in love; flesh stays no further reason;
But, rising at thy name, doth point out thee
As his triumphant prize. Proud of this pride,   10
He is contented thy poor drudge to be,
To stand in thy affairs, fall by thy side.
    No want of conscience hold it that I call
    Her love, for whose dear love I rise and fall.

Butler describes this sonnet in his sub-heading as
'Presumably written by Shakespeare for Mr. W.H. to
give to his (Shakespeare's) mistress, as though written

by himself'. I believe Shakespeare wrote it for himself
and not for Mr. W.H. The words in lines 5 and 6:
. . . 'I do betray
My nobler part to my gross body's treason'
exactly express Shakespeare's reiterated feelings about
his 'affair' with his mistress or any other 'affair' of
that kind. Shakespeare, as I have said before, was a
puritan in the best sense of the word.

57 (35 Q.)

To Mr. W.H.   Shakespeare forgives Mr. W.H. for
having made love to his (Shakespeare's) mistress and
admits that he is himself partly to blame for what has
happened.

No more be griev'd at that which thou hast done,
Roses have thorns and silver fountains mud;
Clouds and eclipses stain both moon and sun,
And loathsome canker lives in sweetest bud.
All men make faults, and even I in this;   5
Authorising thy trespass with compare,
Myself corrupting, salving thy amiss,
Excusing thy sins—more than thy sins are;
For to thy sensual fault I bring in sense—
Thy adverse party is thy Advocate—   10
And 'gainst myself a lawful plea commence:

Such civil war is in my love and hate.
That I an accessory needs must be
To that sweet thief which sourly robs from me.

Line 6. 'Authorising' must be pronounced 'authòr-
ising' to make the line scan.

Line 13. 'Accessory' must be pronounced 'àccessory'
to make the line scan.

Butler says: 'I imagine Shakespeare to be referring
to the fact that he had written sonnets for W.H. to
give the lady as though they were his own.' It certainly looks like it. In any case this sonnet, and the
succeeding three (which are in the same order *inter se*
in the Quarto), conclusively show that Shakespeare
was not angry with his friend, and that he readily
condoned his offence, to which he admits that he was
accessory. This, to my mind, completely disposes of
the generally received idea that the 'dark woman'
episode was the cause of the final rupture (or indeed of
any rupture at all) between the two friends. It also
establishes in my mind the conviction that Butler's
rearrangement of the order of the Sonnets is approxi-
mately correct, and that the sonnets covering the 'dark
woman' episode and some of the others, were misplaced by Thorpe in his edition, either by carelessness
or by design.

58 (40 Q.)

To Mr. W.H.
Shakespeare is still forgiving, but rather sore.

Take all my loves, my love, yea, take them all;
What hast thou then more than thou hadst before?
No love, my love, that thou mayst true love call;
All mine was thine, before thou hadst this more.
Then, if for my love thou my love receivest,   5
I cannot blame thee, for my love thou usedst;
But yet be blam'd, if thou thyself deceivest
By wilful taste of what thyself refusedst.
I do forgive thy robbery, gentle thief,
Although thou steal thee all my poverty;   10
And yet, love knows, it is a greater grief
To bear love's wrong, than hate's known injury.
    Lascivious grace, in whom all ill well shows,
    Kill me with spites; yet we must not be foes.

Lines 6 and 8. Q. reads 'usest' and 'refusest'.
I accept Butler's emendation which he justifies as
follows: 'A man cannot "wilfully" taste what at the
same time he is "refusing". If my text is admitted the
sense will be, "Do not blame me if you find this lady
troublesome; you refused her for some time, and it is
nobody's doing but your own that you now take up

116

with her".' The emendation also gets rid of having four consecutive lines ending in 'est'.

59 (41 Q.)

To Mr. W.H.

Those petty wrongs that liberty commits,
When I am sometimes absent from thy heart,
Thy beauty and thy years full well befits,
For still temptation follows where thou art.
Gentle thou art, and therefore to be won, 5
Beauteous thou art, therefore to be assail'd;
And when a woman woos, what woman's son
Will sourly leave her till she have prevail'd?
Ah me! but yet thou mightst, my sweet, forbear,
And chide thy beauty and thy straying youth, 10
Who lead thee in their riot even there,
Where thou art forc'd to break a two-fold truth;
   Hers, by thy beauty tempting her to thee,
   Thine, by thy beauty being false to me.

Line 1, Q. has 'pretty wrongs'. The emendation is Bell's.

Line 9, Q. reads 'my seate forbear'. The emendation is Malone's.

60 (42 Q.)

To Mr. W.H.

That thou hast her, it is not all my grief,
And yet it may be said I loved her dearly;
That she hath thee, is of my wailing chief,
A loss in love that touches me more nearly.
Loving offenders, thus I will excuse ye: 5
Thou dost love her, because thou know'st I love her;
And for my sake even so doth she abuse me,
Suff'ring my friend for my sake to approve her.
If I lose thee, my loss is my love's gain,
And losing her, my friend hath found that loss;   10
Both find each other, and I lose both twain,
And both for my sake lay on me this cross:
    But here's the joy: my friend and I are one;
    Sweet flatt'ry! then she loves but me alone.

Line 2. Butler remarks: 'one cannot help surmising that with equal truth', it might be said, 'that Shakespeare did *not* love her very dearly'. Which is putting it very mildly.

61 (134 Q.)

To Shakespeare's Mistress.

So, now I have confess'd that he is thine,
And I myself am mortgag'd to thy will;
Myself I'll forfeit, so that other mine
Thou wilt restore, to be my comfort still:
But thou wilt not, nor he will not be free,　　5
For thou art covetous, and he is kind;
He learn'd but, surety-like, to write for me,
Under that bond that him as fast doth bind.
The statute of thy beauty thou wilt take,
Thou usurer, that putt'st forth all to use,　　10
And sue a friend came debtor for my sake;
So him I lose through my unkind abuse.
　　Him have I lost; thou hast both him and me:
　　He pays the whole, and yet am I not free.

62 (133 Q.)

To Shakespeare's Mistress.

Beshrew that heart that makes my heart to groan
For that deep wound it gives my friend and me?
Is't not enough to torture me alone,
But slave to slav'ry my sweet'st friend must be?

Me from myself thy cruel eye hath taken,   5
And my next self thou harder hast engross'd:
Of him, myself, and thee, I am forsaken;
A torment thrice threefold thus to be cross'd.
Prison my heart in thy steel bosom's ward,
But then my friend's heart let my poor heart bail; 10
Who'er keeps me, let my heart be his guard;
Thou canst not then use rigour in my Jail,
   And yet thou wilt; for I, being pent in thee,
   Perforce am thine, and all that is in me.

Evidently the 'dark woman', having achieved her
object, and having subjugated Mr. W.H. is beginning
to torment him as much as she has tormented Shakespeare. Quite the 'Perfect (dark) Lidy', in short.

63 (152 Q.)

To Shakespeare's Mistress.

In loving thee thou know'st I am forsworn,
But thou art twice forsworn, to me love swearing;
In act thy bed-vow broke, and new faith torn,
In vowing new hate after new love bearing.
But why of two oaths' breach do I accuse thee,   5
When I break twenty! I am perjur'd most;
For all my vows are oaths but to misuse thee,

And all my honest faith in thee is lost:
For I have sworn deep oaths of thy deep kindness,
Oaths of thy love, thy truth, thy constancy;　　10
And, to enlighten thee, gave eyes to blindness,
Or made them swear against the thing they see;
　For I have sworn thee fair; more perjur'd I,
　To swear against the truth so foul a lie!

Line 13, Q. reads: 'More perjurde eye'. The emendation is Malone's.

Butler classifies this as 'written by Shakespeare for Mr. W.H. to give to Shakespeare's mistress (who has dismissed him after a brief experience) as though written by himself'.

He goes on to say, 'I agree with Mr. Wyndham in thinking that the connection between Mr. W.H. and Shakespeare's mistress was of short duration. Her love for him had been but recent, and already she was hating him. Whether the disappointment was on her side or on Mr. W.H.'s does not appear, but I suspect it to have been on the lady's, for from sonnet 90 (70 Q.) it appears that Mr. W.H.'s youth had not been stained, and from 114 (94 Q.) we learn that he "does not do the thing" he "most doth show", and that though he moves others he is "himself as stone, unmoved, cold and to temptation slow".'

I agree, of course, that Mr. W.H.'s connection with Shakespeare's mistress was of very short duration. But I do not agree that Shakespeare wrote this sonnet for Mr. W.H. to give to the 'dark woman' as if from himself. I think it was written for himself, simply 'from Shakespeare to his Mistress', and means:

'I know that in loving you I am forsworn (as I am married and my *liaison* with you is illicit and adulterous), but you are twice forsworn, to me and to my friend whom you have tried to take from me. But, when I come to think of it, I am *twenty* times forsworn, in the sense that I have sworn that you are true and constant and kind and loving, and have even persuaded other men to honour you against the evidence of their own senses. In doing this I was perjuring myself every time, for it is a lie to say that you are true and constant and kind and loving. You are in fact the very reverse of all this.'

With this sonnet the 'dark woman' episode comes to an abrupt end. There is no further mention of her in the Sonnets. The friendship between Shakespeare and Mr. W.H. is now renewed, and goes on its course not at all impaired by the relatively trifling disturbance which threatened it.

64 (43 Q.)

To Mr. W.H.
Written in absence.

When most I wink, then do mine eyes best see,
For all the day they view things unrespected;
But when I sleep, in dreams they look on thee,
And, darkly bright, are bright in dark directed.
Then thou, whose shadow shadows doth make
     bright,   5
How would thy shadow's form form happy show
To the clear day with thy much clearer light,
When to unseeing eyes thy shade shines so!
How would, I say, mine eyes be blessed made
By looking on thee in the living day,   10
When in dead night thy fair imperfect shade
Through heavy sleep on sightless eyes doth stay!
  All days are nights to me till I see thee,
  All nights bright days when dreams do show thee
  me.

Line 1. 'Wink' means 'close my eyes'.
Line 13, Q. reads 'All days are nights to see'.
The emendation is Malone's

65 (44 Q.)

To Mr. W.H.
Written in absence.

If the dull substance of my flesh were thought,
Injurious distance should not stop my way;
For then, despite of space, I would be brought,
From limits far remote, where thou dost stay.
No matter then although my foot did stand   5
Upon the farthest earth remov'd from thee;
For nimble thought can jump both sea and land,
As soon as think the place where he would be.
But, ah, thought kills me, that I am not thought,
To leap large lengths of miles when thou art gone, 10
But that, so much of earth and water wrought,
I must attend time's leisure with my moan;
    Receiving nought by elements so slow
    But heavy tears, badges of either's woe.

Line 11, i.e., 'Being so thoroughly compounded of these two ponderous elements' (Malone).

Malone also quotes *Henry V*, iii, i, 'He is pure air and fire, and the dull elements of earth and water never appear in him'. Conf. also *Twelfth Night*, xi, 3: 'Does not our life consist of the four elements?'

66 (45 Q.)

To Mr. W.H.

A continuation of the preceding sonnet.

The other two, slight air and purging fire,
Are both with thee, wherever I abide;
The first my thought, the other my desire,
These present-absent with swift motion slide.
For when these quicker Elements are gone   5
In tender Embassy of love to thee,
My life, being made of four, with two alone
Sinks down to death, oppress'd with melancholy;
Until life's composition be recur'd
By those sweet messengers return'd from thee,   10
Who even but now come back again, assur'd
Of thy fair health, recounting it to me:
    This told, I joy: but then no longer glad,
    I send them back again, and straight grow sad.

Line 8. It is impossible to scan this line, which is a syllable too long, except by cutting out the 'o' in 'melancholy', thus 'melanch'ly'.

67 (46 Q.)

To Mr. W.H. In Absence.

Mine eye and heart are at a mortal war,
How to divide the conquest of thy sight;

Mine eye my heart thy picture's sight would bar,
My heart mine eye the freedom of that right.
My heart doth plead that thou in him dost lie—   5
(A closet never pierc'd with crystal eyes,)
But the defendant doth that plea deny,
And says in him thy fair appearance lies.
To 'cide this title is impannelled
A quest of thoughts, all tenants to the heart   10
And by their verdict is determined.
The clear eye's moiety, and the dear heart's part;
   As thus; mine eye's due is thine outward part,
   And my heart's right thine inward love of heart.

Line 9, Q. reads: 'To side this title'. The emendation is Sewell's.

68 (47 Q.)

To Mr. W.H. In Absence.

Betwixt mine eye and heart a league is took,
And each doth good turns now unto the other:
When that mine eye is famish'd for a look,
Or heart in love with sighs himself doth smother,
With my love's picture then my eye doth feast   5
And to the painted banquet bids my heart;

Another time mine eye is my heart's guest
And in his thoughts of love doth share a part:
So, either by thy picture or my love,
Thyself away art present still with me;　　10
For thou not farther than my thoughts canst move,
And I am still with them and they with thee;
　　Or, if they sleep, thy picture in my sight
　　Awakes my heart to heart's and eye's delight.

69 (48 Q.)

To Mr. W.H. In Absence.

How careful was I when I took my way,
Each trifle under truest bars to thrust,
That to my use it might unused stay
From hands of falsehood, in sure wards of trust!
But thou, to whom my jewels trifles are,　　5
Most worthy comfort, now my greatest grief,
Thou, best of dearest, and mine only care
Art left the prey of every vulgar thief.
Thee have I not lock'd up in any chest,
Save where thou art not, though I feel thou art,　10
Within the gentle closure of my breast,
From whence at pleasure thou mayst come and part;
　　And even thence thou wilt be stol'n, I fear,
　　For Truth proves thievish for a prize so dear.

70 (49 Q.)

To Mr. W.H.
Continuation of preceding Sonnet.

Against that time, if ever that time come,
When I shall see thee frown on my defects,
When as thy love hath cast his utmost sum,
Call'd to that audit by advis'd respects;
Against that time when thou shalt strangely pass, 5
And scarcely greet me with that sun, thine eye,
When love, converted from the thing it was,
Shall reasons find of settled gravity;
Against that time do I ensconce me here
Within the knowledge of mine own desert, 10
And this my hand against myself uprear,
To guard the lawful reasons on thy part:
   To leave poor me thou hast the strength of laws,
   Since why to love I can allege no cause.

Lines 10 and 12. Note 'desert' rhyming with 'part'.

71 (50 Q.)

To Mr. W.H.
Written while Shakespeare was on a Journey.

How heavy do I journey on the way
When what I seek, my weary travel's end,

Doth teach that ease and that repose to say
'Thus far the miles are measur'd from thy friend!'
The beast that bears me, tired with my woe,   5
Plods dully on, to bear that weight in me,
As if by some instinct the wretch did know
His rider lov'd not speed, being made from thee:
The bloody spur cannot provoke him on
That sometimes anger thrüsts into his hide,   10
Which heavily he answers with a groan
More sharp to me than spurring to his side;
   For that same groan doth put this in my mind;
   My grief lies onward, and my joy behind.

Line 6, Q. reads 'Plods duly on'. Malone's emendation.
Line 7, 'instinct' = 'instìnct'.

72 (51 Q.)

To Mr. W.H.
Continuation of preceding Sonnet.

Thus can my love excuse the slow offence
Of my dull bearer when from thee I speed:
From where thou art why should I haste me thence?
Till I return, of posting is no need.

O, what excuse will my poor beast then find,   5
When swift extremity can seem but slow?
Then should I spur, though mounted on the wind,
In winged speed no motion shall I know:
Then can no horse with my desire keep pace;
Therefore desire, of perfect'st love being made,   10
Shall need no dull flesh in his fiery race;
But love, for love, thus shall excuse my jade;
   Since from thee going he went wilful-slow,
   Towards thee I'll run and give him leave to go.

Line 11, Q. reads: 'Shall naigh noe dull flesh in his
fiery race'.

This is obviously corrupt, Various emendations
have been suggested. The one I have adopted is
Butler's.

73 (52 Q.)

To Mr. W.H.
Written after Shakespeare's return.

So am I as the rich, whose blessed key
Can bring him to his sweet up-locked treasure,
The which he will not every hour survey,
For blunting the fine point of seldom pleasure.
Therefore are feasts so seldom and so rare,   5

Since, seldom coming, in the long year set,
Like stones of worth they thinly placed are,
Or captain Jewels in the carcanet,
So is the time that keeps you as my chest,
Or as the wardrobe which the robe doth hide   10
To make some special instant special-blest
By new unfolding his imprison'd pride.
   Blessed are you, whose worthiness gives scope,
   Being had, to triumph, being lack'd, to hope.

74 (53 Q.)

To Mr. W.H.

What is your substance, whereof are you made,
That millions of strange shadows on you tend?
Since every one hath, every one, one shade,
And you, but one, can every shadow lend.
Describe Adonis, and the counterfeit   5
Is poorly imitated after you;
On Helen's cheek all art of beauty set,
And you in *Grecian* tires are painted new:
Speak of the spring and foison of the year,
The one doth shadow of your beauty show,   10
The other as your bounty doth appear;
And you in every blessed shape we know.

In all external grace you have some part,
But you like none, none you, for constant heart.

This is one of the sonnets quoted in Oscar Wilde's
story 'The Portrait of Mr. W.H.', to which I have
already referred, in support of his theory that Mr.
W.H. was an actor.

75 (54 Q.)

O, how much more doth beauty beauteous seem,
By that sweet ornament which truth doth give!
The rose looks fair, but fairer we it deem
For that sweet odour which doth in it live.
The canker-blooms have full as deep a dye   5
As the perfumed tincture of the roses,
Hang on such thorns, and play as wantonly
When summer's breath their masked buds discloses:
But, for their virtue only is their show,
They live unwoo'd, and unrespected fade;   10
Die to themselves. Sweet roses do not so;
Of their sweet deaths are sweetest odours made;
    And so of you, beauteous and lovely youth,
    When that shall fade, by verse distils your truth.

Shakespeare will immortalize his love in his sonnets

76 (55 Q.)

Not marble, nor the gilded monuments
Of princes, shall outlive this powerful rhyme;
But you shall shine more bright in these contents
Than unswept stone, besmear'd with sluttish time,
When wasteful war shall statues overturn,   5
And broils root out the work of masonry,
Nor *Mars* his sword nor war's quick fire shall burn
The living record of your memory.
'Gainst death and all-oblivious enmity
Shall you pace forth; your praise shall still find room
Even in the eyes of all posterity   11
That wear this world out to the ending doom.
  So, till the judgement that yourself arise,
  You live in this, and dwell in lover's eyes.

live in the poems & his eyes forever

Line 1, Q. reads 'Monument'. Malone's emendation.
This magnificent sonnet which has 'Shakespeare'
written all over every line of it, is one of the numerous
sonnets rejected as 'spurious' by Mr. J. M. Robertson.
I can find no flaw in it except the faulty rhyming of
'enmity' and 'posterity' (same consonant sound, *ty*
rhyming to *ty*). But even this stamps it with Shakespeare's mark, for he has similar weak rhymes in various
other sonnets. E.g. he rhymes 'antiquity' with

'iniquity', 'simplicity with authority' and 'impiety' with 'society'. These are all bad rhymes, though they would be accepted as perfect rhymes in French poetry.

In Wilde's 'The Portrait of Mr. W.H.' the theory is put forward that this sonnet was sent by Shakespeare to Mr. W.H. with a copy of *Romeo and Juliet*, and that when Shakespeare speaks of ' "this powerful rhyme" which shall outlive the gilded monuments of princes, and shall preserve for ever "the living record" of Mr. W.H.'s memory', he is not referring to his sonnet but to the play in which, according to Wilde's theory, Mr. W.H. played the part of Juliet. Wilde particularly emphasizes the words:

' 'Gainst death and all-oblivious enmity
Shall you pace forth';

and the last line:

'*You live in this! and dwell in lover's eyes.*'

which he declares can only be explained on the supposition that Mr. W.H. was the boy actor who 'created' the part of Juliet and most of Shakespeare's other heroines.

The theory, as Richard Garnett wrote to Wilde, is

arresting. As I have explained, my chief reason for rejecting it is that I believe Butler to be right in insisting that Shakespeare wrote his sonnets when he was quite young, and before he had written any of his plays. But this does not prevent me from inclining to the belief that Mr. W.H. was a boy actor who played female parts; women, of course, being strictly barred from the stage in Shakespeare's day.

77 (56 Q.)
Concerning Mr. W.H.

Sweet love, renew thy force; be it not said,
Thy edge should blunter be than appetite,
Which but to-day by feeding is allay'd,
To-morrow sharpen'd in his former might:
So, love, be thou, although to-day thou fill   5
Thy hungry eyes, even till they wink with fulness,
To-morrow see again, and do not kill
The spirit of Love with a perpetual dulness.
Let this sad *Int'rim* like the Ocean be
Which parts the shore, where two contracted new 10
Come daily to the banks, that, when they see
Return of love, more blest may be the view;
   Or call it Winter, which, being full of care,

Makes Summer's welcome thrice more wish'd,
more rare.

Line 8. 'Spirit' is here used as one syllable as in
Shakespeare *passim*.

Line 13, Q. reads: 'As cal it Winter'. The emendation is by Tyrwhitt-Malone.

Butler's sub-heading to this sonnet is: 'To Mr. W.H.,
who, satisfied that he has regained his old ascendancy
over Shakespeare, is now neglecting him'. This
smacks to me of Butler and Pauli (see pages 71, 72). It
seems to me that there is no evidence at all that Mr.
W.H. had ever lost his ascendancy over Shakespeare.
The evidence is all in the other direction. I think
Butler mistakes the meaning of this sonnet. Shakespeare, as I take it, is not apostrophizing Mr. W.H.
when he says 'Sweet love renew thy force'; he is
referring to his love for Mr. W.H. It is not to be
supposed again when he says,

'. . . although to-day thou fill
Thy hungry eyes even till they wink with fulness.'

that he means that Mr. W.H. has ever been so much
in love with him (Shakespeare) as this would imply.
The 'hungry eyes' are love's eyes in himself. His
(Shakespeare's) own eyes, in other words.

78 (57 Q.)
To Mr. W.H.

Being your slave, what should I do but tend
Upon the hours and times of your desire?
I have no precious time at all to spend,
Nor services to do, till you require.
Nor dare I chide the world-without-end hour,   5
Whilst I, my sovereign, watch the clock for you,
Nor think the bitterness of absence sour,
When you have bid your servant once adieu;
Nor dare I question with my jealous thought
Where you may be, or your affairs suppose,   10
But, like a sad slave, stay and think of nought,
Save, where you are, how happy you make those.
　So true a fool is love, that in your Will,
　(Though you do anything,) he thinks no ill.

This beautiful and touching sonnet appears to suggest
that Mr. W.H. had been making appointments and not
keeping them.

79 (58 Q.)
To Mr. W.H.
A Continuation of the preceding Sonnet.

That God forbid that made me first your slave,
I should in thought control your times of pleasure,

137

Or at your hand the account of hours to crave,
Being your vassal, bound to stay your leisure!
O, let me suffer, being at your beck;   5
The imprison'd absence of your liberty;
And patience, tame to suff'rance, bide each check,
Without accusing you of injury.
Be where you list, your charter is so strong
That you yourself may privilege your time   10
To what you will; to you it doth belong
Yourself to pardon of self-doing crime.
   I am to wait, though waiting so be hell,
   Not blame your pleasure, be it ill or well.

Line 1. Butler writes: 'The meaning is, "Let me suffer the imprisonment of being kept at home waiting for you while you take your liberty and absent yourself (after having promised to come to see me)".' Pauli again, I take it! But there is more warrant for Butler's inference here than in the case of the last sonnet but one.

80 (59 Q.)

To Mr. W.H.

If there be nothing new, but that which is
Hath been before, how are our brains beguil'd,

Which, labouring for invention, bear amiss
The second burthen of a former child!
O, that record could with a backward look,   5
Even of five hundred courses of the sun,
Show me your image in some antique book,
Since mind at first in character was done.
That I might see what the old world could say
To this composed wonder of your frame;   10
Whether we're mended, or whêr better they,
Or whether revolution be the same,
    O, sure I am, the wits of former days
    To subjects worse have given admiring praise.

Line 5, 'record' = 'recòrd'.

Line 11, Q. has: 'Whether we are mended, or whether better they'.

This reading which makes the line two syllables too long and produces an appalling effect, appears to be generally accepted. Butler follows it, and I searched vainly for an alternative reading till I found what appears above in Dyce's edition. The word 'wher', for whether is often used in Shakespeare, as Dyce points out in a note to *Troilus and Cressida*. Anyhow, it makes the line scan, which is the main thing from the point of view of a poet.

81 (60 Q.)

To Mr. W.H.

Like as the waves make t'wards the pebbled shore,
So do our minutes hasten to their end;
Each changing place with that which goes before,
In sequent toil all forwards do contend.
Nativity, once in the main of light,   5
Crawls to maturity, wherewith being crown'd,
Crooked eclipses 'gainst his glory fight,
And Times, that gave, doth now his gift confound.
Time doth transfix the flourish set on youth,
And delves the parallels in beauty's brow;   10
Feeds on the rarities of nature's truth,
And nothing stands but for his scythe to mow:
   And yet, to times in hope my verse shall stand,
   Praising thy worth, despite his cruel hand.

82 (61 Q.)

To Mr. W.H.

Is it thy will thy Image should keep open
My heavy eyelids to the weary night?
Dost thou desire my slumbers should be broken,
While shadows like to thee do mock my sight?

Is it thy spirit that thou send'st from thee   5
So far from home into my deeds to pry,
To find out shames and idle hours in me,
The scope and tenour of thy Jealousy?
O, no! thy love, though much, is not so great:
It is my love that keeps mine eye awake;   10
Mine own true love that dost my rest defeat,
To play the watchman ever for thy sake:
    For thee watch I whilst thou dost wake elsewhere,
    From me far off, with others all too near.

Line 5. 'Spirit' here is two syllables. Shakespeare
usually makes it one, as in sonnet 77 (56 Q.).

83 (62 Q.)

To Mr. W.H.

Sin of self-love possesseth all mine eye,
And all my soul, and all my every part;
And for this sin there is no remedy,
It is so grounded inward in my heart,
Methinks no face so gracious is as mine,   5
No shape so true, no truth of such account;
And for myself mine own worth do define,
As I all other in all worths surmount.

But when my glass shows me myself indeed,
Beated and chopp'd with tann'd antiquity,   10
Mine own self-love quite contrary I read;
Self so self-loving were iniquity.
  'Tis thee (myself) that for myself I praise,
  Painting my age with beauty of thy days.

Line 10. Here again we have Shakespeare referring
to his advanced age. For my reasons (which I share
with Butler) for supposing that Shakespeare was really
very young when he wrote these sonnets, see my remarks on Sonnet 47 (138 Q.). Further on in this book,
when dealing with Sonnets 127 (107 Q.) and 148
(125 Q.), I will quote what I take to be Butler's convincing proof that the latest of these sonnets to, or
concerning, Mr. W.H. was written towards the end
of 1588 when Shakespeare was about twenty-four and
a half years old.

84 (63 Q.)

To Mr. W.H.

Against my love shall be, as I am now,
With Time's injurious hand crush'd and o'er worn:
When hours have drained his blood, and fill'd his
  brow

With lines and wrinkles; when his youthful morn
Hath travell'd on to age's steepy night;   5
And all those beauties whereof now he's king,
Are vanishing or vanish'd out of sight,
Stealing away the treasure of his spring;
For such a time do I now fortify
Against confounding Age, his cruel knife   10
That he shall never cut from memory
My sweet love's beauty, though my lover's life:
   His beauty shall in these black lines be seen,
   And they shall live, and he in them still green.

On the question of Shakespeare's age when he wrote
this sonnet I refer back to my remarks on the preceding sonnet. It has just occurred to me that Barn-
field who, when he wrote 'The Affectionate Shepherd'
was not more than twenty, writes that poem in the
person of an old man.

85 (64 Q.)

To Mr. W.H.

When I have seen by Time's fell hand defac'd
The rich-proud cost of outworn buri'd age;
When sometimes lofty towers I see down-raz'd,

And brass eternal slave to mortal rage;
When I have seen the hungry Ocean gain   5
Advantage on the Kingdom of the shore,
And the firm soil win of the wat'ry main,
Increasing store with loss and loss with store;
When I have seen such interchange of state,
Or state itself confounded to decay;   10
Ruin hath taught me thus to ruminate,
That Time will come and take my love away,
 This thought is as a death, which cannot choose
 But weep to have that which it fears to lose.

86 (65 Q.)

To Mr. W.H.

Since brass, nor stone, nor earth, nor boundless sea,
But sad mortality, o'er-sways their power,
How with this rage shall beauty hold a plea
Whose action is no stronger than a flower?
O, how shall summer's honey breath hold out   5
Against the wrackful siege of batt'ring days,
When rocks impregnable are not so stout,
Nor gates of steel so strong, but Time decays?
O fearful meditation where, alack,
Shall Time's best Jewel from Time's quest lie hid? 10

O, what strong hand can hold his swift foot back?
Or who his spoil of beauty can forbid?
 O, none, unless this miracle have might,
 That in black ink my love may still shine bright.

Line 10, Q. reads 'Time's chest'. The emendation
is by Theobald, at first approved; but afterwards rejected by Malone.

Line 11, Q. reads 'Or what strong hand'. I adopt
Butler's emendation.

Line 12, Q. reads 'Or who his spoile or beautie'.
The emendation is Malone's.

87 (66 Q.)

To Mr. W.H.

Tir'd with all these, for restful death I cry,—
As, to behold desert a beggar born,
And needy Nothing trimm'd in jollity,
And purest faith unhappily forsworn,
And gilded honour shamefully misplac'd,   5
And maiden virtue rudely strumpeted,
And right perfection wrongfully disgrac'd,
And strength by limping sway disabled,
And art made tongue-tied by authority,
And Folly, Doctor-like, controlling skill,   10

And simple Truth miscall'd Simplicity,
And captive good attending Captain Ill:
  T,ir'd with all these, from these would I be gone,
  Save that, to die, I leave my love alone.

Line 8. In order to make this line scan it is necessary
to make 'disabled' into four syllables, thus 'disabelèd'.
This, however, appears to me quite legitimate.

88 (67 Q.)

To Mr. W.H. Lamenting the bad company he has been keeping.

Ah, wherefore with infection should he live,
And with his presence grace impiety,
That sin by him advantage should achieve,
And lace itself with his society?
Why should false painting imitate his cheek,   5
And steal dead seeming of his inward hue?
Why should poor beauty indirectly seek
Roses of shadow, since his Rose is true?
Why should he live, now Nature bankrupt is,
Beggar'd of blood to blush through lively veins? 10
For she hath no exchequer now but his,
And, prov'd of many, lives upon his gains,
  O, him she stores, to show what wealth she had
  In days long since, before these last so bad.

Line 12, Q. reads 'proud of many'. I adopt Capell's emendation.

This sonnet is surely a rebuke to those who persist in finding evil in Shakespeare's devotion to Mr. W.H. If we are to accept the suggestion that Shakespeare had a 'guilty passion' for Mr. W.H., we must write him down also a contemptible hypocrite in face of this sonnet. Not that this would be any bar to the 'facts of life' school, represented by the late Arnold Bennett and Frank Harris, who see evil in everything and are unable to believe in the possibility of human goodness and purity. But at least one would suppose that such a consideration might weigh with those who not only admire Shakespeare as an incomparable poet, but are also anxious to think the best of him. I include in the category of those who wrong Shakespeare on this point, not only those who openly accuse him, but also those who refuse to discuss the subject at all, thereby implying that it will not bear looking into.

89 (68 Q.)

To Mr. W.H.

Thus is his cheek the map of days outworn,
When beauty lived and died as flow'rs do now,

Before these bastard signs of fair were born,
Or durst inhabit on a living brow;
Before the golden tresses of the dead, 5
The right of sepulchres, were shorn away,
To live a second life on second head;
Ere beauty's dead fleece made another gay:
In him those holy antique hours are seen,
Without all ornaments himself and true, 10
Making no summer of another's green,
Robbing no old to dress his beauty new;
   And him as for a map doth Nature store,
   To show false Art what beauty was of yore.

Line 10, Q. reads, 'Without all ornament, it selfe
and true'. The reading here given was conjectured by
Malone, but he did not adopt it.

90 (69 Q.)

To Mr. W.H.

Those parts of thee that the world's eye doth view
Want nothing that the thought of hearts can mend;
All tongues, the voice of souls, give thee that due,
Utt'ring bare truth, even so as foes Commend.
Thy outward thus with outward praise is crown'd; 5

But those same tongues, that give thee so thine own,
In other accents do this praise confound
By seeing farther than the eye hath shown.
They look into the beauty of thy mind,
And that, in guess, they measure by thy deeds;   10
Then, churls, their thoughts, although their eyes
    were kind,
To thy fair flow'r add the rank smell of weeds:
  But why thy odour matcheth not thy show,
  The solve is this, that thou dost common grow.

Line 3, Q. reads, 'give that end', which is obviously wrong because 'end' does not rhyme with 'view'. The emendation is Malone's.

Line 14, Q. reads 'the solye is this', and in 'The Temple' and many other editions it is printed 'soil'. But this makes no sense, and I adopt Malone's emendation, 'solve'. The sense plainly is: 'The reason why your odour (that is your reputation) does not conform with the beauty of your outward appearance is that you grow "common", that is to say, you cheapen yourself by keeping bad company'.

In my edition (1927) of Butler's *Shakespeare's Sonnets Reconsidered* a footnote states that Richard Garnett, in a letter to Butler about Butler's book on the Sonnets, suggested reading 'foil' for 'soil', and that Butler in a letter dated 15th December, 1899, accepted this emendation. But 'soil' is still the reading given in this (1927) edition of Butler's book. In any case, I cannot accept Richard Garnett's emendation as a good one. I fail to see that 'foil' makes any better sense than 'soil'. Accordingly, I adopt 'solve', which is the version adopted by Dyce.

91 (70 Q.)

To Mr W.H., defending him against the detractors mentioned in the preceding sonnet.

That thou art blam'd shall not be thy defect,
For slander's mark was ever yet the fair;
The ornament of beauty is suspect,
A crow that flies in heaven's sweetest air.
So thou be good, slander doth but approve   5
Thy worth the greater, being woo'd oftime;
For canker vice the sweetest buds doth love,
And thou present'st a pure unstained prime.
Thou hast pass'd by the ambush of young days,
Or not assail'd, or victor being charg'd;   10
Yet this thy praise cannot be so thy praise,
To tie up envy, evermore enlarg'd:
   If some suspect of ill mask'd not thy show,
   Then thou alone kingdoms of hearts shouldst owe.

Line 3. The word 'suspect' is here a substantive and = 'suspicion'; and the same applies to the word, used again, in line 13.

Line 6, Q. reads, 'Their worth the greater being woo'd of time'. The Cambridge edition states that the emendation to 'oftime' has been suggested, but it had not, I believe, been adopted before Butler took it.

Line 10, Q. reads, 'Either not assailed'; the emendation, for scansion's sake, is mine.

In this sonnet, Shakespeare, as it seems to me, answers by anticipation Butler's libels on, and abuse of, Mr. W.H. Shakespeare says to Mr. W.H. in effect: 'You are not to be blamed because you are slandered. Beautiful people are invariably slandered. Virtuous as you are, this kind of evil speaking only adds to your worth. Vice always tries to corrupt innocence and sweetness like yours, but you have passed unscathed through all sorts of temptations. If some suspicion of evil did not attach to you, it would be against all experience of what invariably happens to the lovely and innocent.' It is true that Shakespeare afterwards quarrelled with Mr. W.H., but that he wrote of him in this beautiful and touching way some time after the 'Dark Woman' episode should never be forgotten. Again I take it that this sonnet is an overwhelming reply to those who impute 'guilt' to

Shakespeare in his relations with Mr. W.H. as well as to those who insult him by treating the whole question as undiscussable.

92 (71 Q.)

To Mr. W.H.

No longer mourn for me when I am dead
Than you shall hear the surly sullen bell
Give warning to the world that I am fled
From this vile world, with vilest worms to dwell:
Nay, if you read this line, remember not   5
The hand that writ it; for I love you so,
That I in your sweet thoughts would be forgot,
If thinking on me then should make you woe.
O, if, I say, you look upon this verse
When I perhaps compounded am with clay,   10
Do not so much as my poor name rehearse,
But let your love even with my life decay;
　　Lest the wise world should look into your moan,
　　And mock you with me after I am gone.

93 (72 Q.)

To Mr. W.H.

O, lest the world should task you to recite
What merit liv'd in me, that you should love

After my death, dear love, forget me quite,
For you in me can nothing worthy prove;
Unless you would devise some virtuous lie,　　5
To do more for me than mine own desert,
And hang more praise upon deceasèd I
Than niggard truth would willingly impart:
O, lest your true love may seem false in this,
That you for love speak well of me untrue,　　10
My name be buri'd where my body is,
And live no more to shame nor me nor you.
　　For I am sham'd by that which I bring forth,
　　And so should you, to love things nothing worth.

Lines 6 and 8. Note 'desert' rhyming with 'impart'.
Line 10, 'untrue'='untruly'.

94 (73 Q.)

To Mr. W.H.

That time of year thou mayst in me behold
When yellow leaves, or none, or few, do hang
Upon those boughs which shake against the cold,
Bare ruin'd choirs, where late the sweet birds sang.
In me thou see'st the twilight of such day　　5
As after Sunset fadeth in the West;

Which by and by black night doth take away,
Death's second self, that seals up all in rest.
In me, thou see'st the glowing of such fire,
That on the ashes of his youth doth lie,   10
As the death-bed whereon it must expire,
Consum'd with that which it was nourish'd by.
 This thou perceiv'st, which makes thy love more
  strong,
 To love that well which thou must leave ere long.

Line 4. The Q. has 'ru'nd quiers'.

95 (74 Q.)

To Mr. W.H.

But he contented: when that fell arrest
Without all bail shall carry me away,
My life hath in this line some interest,
Which for memorial still with thee shall stay.
When thou reviewest this, thou dost review 5
The very part was consecrate to thee:
The earth can have but earth, which is his due;
My spirit is thine, the better part of me:
So, then, thou hast but lost the dregs of life,

The prey of worms, my body being dead;   10
The coward conquest of a wretch's knife,
Too base of thee to be remembered.
   The worth of that, is that which it contains,
   And that is this, and this with thee remains.

Line 8, 'spirit' here is one syllable as nearly always
in Shakespeare.

96 (75 Q.)

To Mr. W.H.

So are you to my thoughts as food to life,
Or as sweet-season'd show'rs are to the ground;
And for the peace of you I hold such strife
As 'twixt a miser and his wealth is found;
Now proud as an enjoyer, and anon   5
Doubting the filching age will steal his treasure;
Now counting best to be with you alone,
Then better'd that the world may see my pleasure:
Sometime all full with feasting on your sight,
And by and by clean starved for a look;   10
Possessing or pursuing no delight,
Save what is had or must from you be took.

Thus do I pine and surfeit day by day,
Or gluttoning on all, or all away.

Line 3, Q. reads, 'And for the peace of you'. Butler adopts Staunton's emendation 'prize' for 'peace'. I stick to the Quarto, following Malone, who however declares that the context would seem to require 'price' or 'sake'. But as Malone, after some hesitation, decided, I think that obviously Shakespeare intended an antithesis between 'peace' and 'strife'.

97 (76 Q.)

To Mr. W.H., probably written in December 1585

Why is my verse so barren of new pride,
So far from variation or quick change?
Why, with the time, do I not glance aside
To new-found methods and to compounds strange?
Why write I still all one, ever the same, 5
And keep invention in a noted weed,
That every word doth almost tell my name,
Showing their birth, and where they did proceed?
O, know, sweet love, I always write of you,
And you and love are still my argument; 10
So all my best is dressing old words new,
Spending again what is already spent:

For as the sun is daily new and old,
So is my love still telling what is told.

Line 6. 'Keep invention in a noted weed.' 'Weed' here means 'garment' (as before, in sonnet 2). The sense of this and preceding lines is: 'Why do I go on using the same invariable method in my writing, and continually keep invention in a well-known and easily recognized form (i.e., the sonnet form)?'

This is a most important sonnet for the support it gives to the theory which, with Butler, I adopt, that Shakespeare's Sonnets were the first things he ever wrote. He says in effect: 'People must be surprised that I never launch out into new fields by writing in other forms, and that I stick entirely to sonnets about you, but the fact is I can write only of you over and over again, and all my best is a variation of the same old theme.' How can this square with the theory, generally received and supported by the great mass of 'eminent Shakespearian scholars', that Shakespeare was at least twenty-seven or twenty-eight when he wrote the Sonnets, and that he had then already written *Lucrece*, *Venus and Adonis* and the earlier plays?

This sonnet is reckoned by Butler to be the last sonnet of the series written in 1585. He dates it 'probably December'.

98 (77 Q.)

To Mr. W.H. with a present of a book of tablets. 1586.

Thy glass will show thee how thy beauties wear,
Thy dial how thy precious minutes waste;
These vacant leaves thy mind's imprint will bear,
And of this book this learning mayst thou taste.
The wrinkles which thy glass will truly show,   5
Of mouthed graves will give thee memory;
Thou by thy dial's shady stealth mayst know
Time's thievish progress to eternity.
Look, what thy memory cannot contain,
Commit to these waste blanks, and thou shalt find 10
Those children nurs'd, deliver'd from thy brain,
To take a new acquaintance of thy mind.
   These offices, so oft as thou wilt look,
   Shall profit thee, and much enrich thy book.

Line 3, Q. reads, 'The vacant leaves'. Emendation suggested by Malone but not adopted by him. Conf. Line 10, 'commit to these waste blanks', referring, evidently, to the empty pages of the book of tablets which accompanied the sonnet when Shakespeare sent it to Mr. W.H.

According to Butler's reckoning, this sonnet was sent to Mr. W.H. on January 1st, 1586.

99 (78 Q.)

To Mr. W.H. who, apparently, has now inspired other
poets to write about him.

So oft have I invok'd thee for my Muse,
And found such fair assistance in my verse,
As every *Alien* pen hath got my use,
And under thee their poesy disperse.
Thine eyes, that taught the dumb on high to sing,   5
And heavy ignorance aloft to fly,
Have added feathers to the learned's wing,
And given grace a double Majesty.
Yet be most proud of that which I compile,
Whose influence is thine, and born of thee: 10
In others' works thou dost but mend the style,
And Arts with thy sweet graces graced be;
    But thou art all my art, and dost advance
    As high as learning my rude ignorance.

Line 3. Wilde suspects a pun in this line, in the last
word on the name 'Hughes' or 'Hews', and he points
out that in various other sonnets there are similar
'puns' on the words 'use' and 'usury'. This is ingenious, but I am afraid that it is not very convincing
when one comes to look closely into it.

Butler's comment on line 5 and what follows is:

'Surely these lines afford considerable ground for thinking that Shakespeare had not written at all before falling in with Mr. W.H. Conf. 'By heaven I do love; and it hath taught me to rhyme (*Love's Labour's Lost*, IV, iii—the opening speech)'. I agree.

100 (79 Q.)

Mr. W.H.
A continuation of the preceding sonnet.

Whilst I alone did call upon thy aid,
My verse alone had all thy gentle grace;
But now my gracious numbers are decay'd,
And my sick Muse doth give another place.
I grant, sweet love, thy lovely argument   5
Deserves the travail of a worthier pen;
Yet what of thee thy Poet doth invent
He robs thee of, and pays it thee again.
He lends thee virtue, and he stole that word
From thy behaviour; beauty doth he give,   10
And found it in thy cheek: he can afford
No praise to thee but what in thee doth live.
   Then thank him not for that which he doth say,
   Since what he owes thee thou thyself dost pay.

It is impossible to guess who was the poet here

referred to. Wilde, after first suggesting Chapman, finally settles on Marlowe. But Wilde's theory depends upon his hypothesis that Mr. W.H. was the boy actor who acted the female parts in Shakespeare's plays, and he suggests that Marlowe 'lured away' Mr. W.H. from Shakespeare's company of players to play the part of Piers Gaveston in his *Edward II*. All this is very plausible and ingenious, and it is only on the question of dates, already discussed, that I definitely reject it.

101 (80 Q.)

To Mr. W.H., a continuation of the two preceding sonnets.

O, how I faint when I of you do write,
Knowing a better spirit doth use your name,
And in the praise thereof spends all his might,
To make me tongue-ti'd, speaking of your fame!
But since your worth, wide as the Ocean is,   5
The humble as the proudest sail doth bear,
My saucy bark inferior far to his
On your broad main doth wilfully appear.
Your shallowest help will hold me up afloat,
While he upon your soundless deep doth ride;   10
Or, being wreck'd, I am a worthless boat,
He of tall building and of goodly pride:

161

Then if he thrive and I be cast away,
The worst was this; my love was my decay.

This sonnet again is strong proof that Shakespeare
was very young when he wrote it. Would he have
ever admitted that his 'saucy bark' was 'inferior far'
to that of any other poet then living, after he had
written *Venus and Adonis, Lucrece, Love's Labour's Lost,
The Two Gentlemen of Verona* and *Romeo and Juliet*? I
say, certainly not. The words of the sonnet are, on
the other hand, peculiarly and modestly and appropriate in the mouth, or from the pen, of a young poet who
is writing his first volume of (as yet unpublished) verse.

102 (81 Q.)

To Mr. W.H.

Or shall I live your epitaph to make,
Or you survive when I in earth am rotten;
From hence your memory death cannot take,
Although in me each part will be forgotten,
Your name from hence immortal life shall have,   5
Though I, once gone, to all the world must die:
The earth can yield me but a common grave,
When you entombed in men's eyes shall lie.

Your monument shall be my gentle verse,
Which eyes not yet created shall o'er-read;   10
And tongues to be your being shall rehearse,
When all the breathers of this world are dead:
    You still shall live—such virtue hath my pen—
    Where breath most breathes, even in the mouths
        of men.

Line 1, 'Or' = 'Whether'.

103 (82 Q.)

To Mr. W.H.

I grant thou wert not married to my Muse,
And therefore mayst without attaint o'erlook
The dedicated words which writers use
Of their fair subject, blessing every book.
Thou art as fair in knowledge as in hue,   5
Finding thy worth a limit past my praise,
And therefore art enforc'd to seek anew
Some fresher stamp of the time-bett'ring days.
And do so, love; yet when they have devis'd
What strained touches Rhetoric can lend,   10
Thou truly fair wert truly sympathiz'd
In true plain words by thy true-telling friend;
    And their gross painting might be better us'd
    Where cheeks need blood; in thee it is abus'd.

104 (83 Q.)

To Mr. W.H.

I never saw that you did painting need,
And therefore to your fair no painting set;
I found, or thought I found, you did exceed
The barren tender of a Poet's debt:
And therefore have I slept in your report, 5
That you yourself, being extant, well might show
How far a modern quill doth come too short,
Speaking of worth, what worth in you doth grow.
This silence for my sin you did impute,
Which shall be most my glory, being dumb; 10
For I impair not beauty being mute,
When others would give life and bring a tomb
 There lives more life in one of your fair eyes
 Than both your Poets can in praise devise.

Butler's sub-heading to this sonnet is as follows:
'To Mr. W.H. Shakespeare's jealousy has led him to
leave off writing. Mr. W.H., however, being "fond
on praise", has again cajoled him.' I agree that line
5 indicates that there had been an interval of silence,
but where Butler gets his evidence that Mr. W.H.
had 'again cajoled Shakespeare' I am at a loss to under-
stand. I suggest that here again he is reading his own

personal experiences into the story of Shakespeare and Mr. W.H. His *parti pris* to attack the character and conduct of Mr. W.H. is astonishing, and inexplicable, except on the assumption which I adopt.

105 (84 Q.)

To Mr. W.H.

Who is it that says most? which can say more
Than this rich praise, that you alone are you?
In whose confine immured is the store
Which should example where your equal grew?
Lean penury within that pen doth dwell   5
That to his subject lends not some small glory;
But he that writes of you, if he can tell
That you are you, so dignifies his story.
Let him but copy what in you is writ,
Not making gross what nature made so clear,   10
And such a counterpart shall fame his wit,
Making his style admired every where.
    You to your beauteous blessings add a curse.
    Being fond on praise, which makes your praises
    worse.

Lines 1-4, Q. has no notes of interrogation, but they are obviously needed. I have added them, following Malone, as to the two first, and Staunton as to the third.

Line 10, Q. reads, 'Not making worse'. I adopt Butler's emendation suggested by Staunton.

Line 14. 'Being fond on praise' means, of course, 'being fond of praise'. Conf. 'We are such stuff as dreams are made on'.—*The Tempest*, IV, i.

106 (85 Q.)

To Mr. W.H.

My tongue-ti'd Muse in manners holds her still,
While comments of your praise, richly compil'd,
Rehearse thy Character with golden quill,
And precious phrase by all the Muses fil'd.
I think good thoughts, whilst other write good
  words,   5
And, like unletter'd clerk, still cry 'Amen'
To every Hymn that able spirit affords,
In polish'd form of well refined pen.
Hearing you prais'd, I say ' 'tis so, 'tis true',
And to the most of praise add something more; 10
But that is in my thought, whose love to you,
Though words come hindmost, holds his rank
  before.

Then others for the breath of words respect,
Me for my dumb thoughts, speaking in effect.

Line 3, Q. reads 'Reserve'. I adopt 'Rehearse' which
is mentioned in the Cambridge edition as having been
proposed.

107 (86 Q.)

To Mr. W.H.

Was it the proud full sail of his great verse,
Bound for the prize of all-too-precious you,
That did my ripe thoughts in my brain inhearse,
Making their tomb the womb wherein they grew?
Was it his spirit, by spirits taught to write   5
Above a mortal pitch, that struck me dead?
No, neither he, nor his compeers by night
Giving him aid, my verse astonished.
He, nor that affable familiar ghost
Which nightly gulls him with intelligence,   10
As victors, of my silence cannot boast;
I was not sick of any fear from thence:
But when your countenance fill'd up his line,
Then lack'd I matter; that enfeebled mine.

The rival poet referred to by Shakespeare is perhaps

Chapman. Wilde in his 'The Portrait of Mr. W.H.' writes as follows:

'It is in reference to this (i.e. W.H.'s abandonment of Shakespeare's Company to play at a rival Theatre probably in some of Chapman's plays) that in the great sonnet on Chapman, Shakespeare said to Willie Hughes—"But when your countenance filled up his line, then lacked I matter; that enfeebled mine". The expression, "When your countenance filled up his line", referring obviously to the beauty of the young actor giving life and reality . . . to Chapman's verse.' —Later in his book Wilde, through one of the other characters in the story speaks thus: 'Finally I came to the conclusion that Cyril Graham had been wrong in regarding the rival dramatist of the 86th sonnet as Chapman. It was obviously Marlowe who was alluded to. [Everything he advanced in any discussion was always 'obvious' to Wilde! . . .]

Marlowe was clearly the rival dramatist of whom Shakespeare spoke in such laudatory terms: and that

. . . "Affable familiar ghost
Who nightly gulls him with intelligence"

was the Mephistopheles of his Doctor Faustus.'

108 (87 Q.)

To Mr. W.H.

Shakespeare, whose jealousy has been more and more evident in the last few preceding sonnets, now declares that all is over between him and his friend, and bids him farewell for ever.

Farewell! thou art too dear for my possessing,
And like enough thou know'st thy estimate:
The Charter of thy worth gives thee releasing;
My bonds in thee are all determinate.
For how do I hold thee but by thy granting?   5
And for that riches where is my deserving?
The cause of this fair gift in me is wanting,
And so my patent back again is swerving.
Thyself thou gav'st, thy own worth then not
    knowing,
Or me, to whom thou gav'st it, else mistaking;   10
So thy great gift, upon misprision growing,
Comes home again, on better judgement making,
    Thus have I had thee, as a dream doth flatter,
    In sleep a king, but waking no such matter.

Wilde has the following in his 'Portrait of Mr. W.H.':
'That Shakespeare had the legal right to retain Willie

Hughes in his company is evident from Sonnet 87'.

Wilde then quotes the sonnet italicizing the words *'Charter of thy worth'* and *'bonds'* and the line

'And so my patent back again is swerving'.

He goes on: 'But him whom he could not hold by love he would not hold by force. Willie Hughes became a member of Lord Pembroke's company, etc.'

109 (88 Q.)

To Mr. W.H.

When thou shalt be dispos'd to set me light,
And place my merit in the eye of scorn,
Upon thy side against myself I'll fight
And prove thee virtuous, though thou art forsworn.
With mine own weakness being best acquainted, 5
Upon thy part I can set down a story
Of faults conceal'd, wherein I am attainted,
That thou in losing me shalt win much glory:
And I by this will be a gainer too;
For bending all my loving thoughts on thee, 10
The injuries that to myself I do,
Doing thee vantage, double-vantage me.
 Such is my love, to thee I so belong,
 That for thy right myself will bear all wrong.

Shakespeare, being now anxious to make up the quarrel, declares that he is ready to take all the blame for it on himself. He is evidently very unhappy, and the following five sonnets are all in the same vein of affectionate bitterness.

110 (89 Q.)

Say that thou didst forsake me for some fault,
And I will comment upon that offence:
Speak of my lameness, and I straight will halt,
Against thy reasons, making no defence,
Thou canst not, love, disgrace me half so ill,   5
To set a form upon desired change,
As I'll myself disgrace; knowing thy will,
I will acquaintance strangle and look strange;
Be absent from thy walks; and in my tongue
Thy sweet beloved name no more shall dwell,   10
Lest I, too much profane, should do it wrong,
And haply of our old acquaintance tell.
   For thee, against myself I'll vow debate,
   For I must ne'er love him whom thou dost hate.

Line 3. Butler has this comment: 'This line seems to imply that the lameness of which Shakespeare spoke in sonnet 37 has not entirely left him. It suggests "I am no longer lame, but if you choose to say that I still go more or less halt, I will halt at once." Probably he still halted a little.' As I have already said, I agree with Malone that the 'lameness' alluded to here and in sonnet 37 must not be taken literally.

III (91 Q.)

To Mr. W.H.

Then hate me when thou wilt; if ever, now;
Now, while the world is bent my deeds to cross,
Join with the spite of fortune, make me bow,
And do not drop in for an after-loss:
O, do not, when my heart hath 'scap'd this sorrow, 5
Come in the rearward of a conquer'd woe;
Give not a windy night a rainy morrow,
To linger out a purpos'd overthrow.
If thou wilt leave me, do not leave me last,
When other petty griefs have done their spite, 10
But in the onset come: so shall I taste
At first the very worst of fortune's might;
   And other strains of woe, which now seem woe,
   Compar'd with loss of thee will not seem so.

112 (91 Q.)

Some glory in their birth, some in their skill,
Some in their wealth, some in their body's force;
Some in their garments, though new-fangled ill;
Some in their Hawks and Hounds, some in their
    Horse;
And every humour hath his adjunct pleasure,   5
Wherein it finds a joy above the rest:
But these particulars are not my measure;
All these I better in one general best.
Thy love is better than high birth to me,
Richer than wealth, prouder than garments' cost, 10
Of more delight than Hawks or Horses be;
And having thee, of all men's pride I boast:
    Wretched in this alone, that thou mayst take
    All this away and me most wretched make.

113 (92 Q.)

To Mr. W.H.

But do thy worst to steal thyself away,
For term of life thou art assured mine;
And life no longer than thy love will stay,
For it depends upon that love of thine.
Then need I not to fear the worst of wrongs,   5
When in the least of them my life hath end.

I see a better state to me belongs
Than that which on thy humour doth depend:
Thou canst not vex me with inconstant mind,
Since that my life on thy revolt doth lie.　　　10
O, what a happy title do I find,
Happy to have thy love, happy to die!
　　But what's so blessed-fair that fears no blot?
　　Thou mayst be false, and yet I know it not.

114 (93 Q.)

To Mr. W.H.

So shall I live, supposing thou art true,
Like a deceived husband; so love's face
May still seem love to me, though alter'd new;
Thy looks with me, thy heart in other place:
For there can live no hatred in thine eye,　　　5
Therefore in that I cannot know thy change.
In many's looks the false heart's history
Is writ in moods and frowns and wrinkles strange,
But heav'n in thy creation did decree
That in thy face sweet love should ever dwell;　　　10
Whate'er thy thoughts or thy heart's workings be,
Thy looks should nothing thence but sweetness tell.
　　How like Eve's apple doth thy beauty grow,
　　If thy sweet virtue answer not thy show!

115 (94 Q.)

To Mr. W.H.

They that have power to hurt and will do none,
That do not do the thing they most do show,
Who, moving others, are themselves as stone,
Unmoved, cold, and to temptation slow—
They rightly do inherit heaven's graces   5
And husband nature's riches from expense;
They are the Lords and owners of their faces,
Others but stewards of their excellence.
The summer's flow'r is to the summer sweet,
Though to itself it only live and die: 10
But if that flow'r with base infection meet,
The basest weed outbraves his dignity:
    For sweetest things turn sourest by their deeds;
    Lilies that fester smell far worse than weeds.

Shakespeare in this and the two succeeding sonnets, under cover of most affectionate and loving words, gets in some pretty hard knocks at Mr. W.H. who is now, according to Shakespeare's account, behaving very badly. But it is fair to remember that Shakespeare wrote all this group of sonnets under the influence of jealousy and soreness. His remonstrances and reproaches evidently produced a break between the friends, for it is quite plain that there is a considerable gap between sonnets 117 (96 Q.) and 118 (97 Q.), when the quarrel is made up and Shakespeare returns to his former serenity.

116 (95 Q.)

To Mr. W.H.

How sweet and lovely dost thou make the shame
Which, like a canker in the fragrant rose,
Doth spot the beauty of thy budding name!
O, in what sweets dost thou thy sins inclose!
That tongue that tells the story of thy days,   5
Making lascivious comments on thy sport,
Cannot dispraise but in a kind of praise;
Naming thy name blesses an ill report.
O, what a mansion have those vices got
Which for their habitation chose out thee,   10
Where beauty's veil doth cover every blot,
And all things turn to fair that eyes can see!
    Take heed, dear heart, of this large privilege;
    The hardest knife ill us'd doth lose his edge.

117 (96 Q.)

To Mr. W.H.

Some say thy fault is youth, some wantonness,
Some say thy grace is youth and gentle sport;
Both grace and faults are lov'd of more and less;
Thou mak'st faults graces that to thee resort.
As on the finger of a throned Queen   5
The basest jewel will be well esteem'd,
So are those errors that in thee are seen
To truths translated and for true things deem'd.
How many Lambs might the stern Wolf betray,
If like a Lamb he could his looks translate!   10
How many gazers mightst thou lead away,
If thou wouldst use the strength of all thy state!
    But do not so; I love thee in such sort
    As, thou being mine, mine is thy good report.

118 (97 Q.)

To Mr. W.H.   Autumn, 1586.

How like a winter hath my absence been
From thee, the pleasure of the fleeting year:
What freezings have I felt, what dark days seen!
What old December's bareness every where!

And yet this time remov'd was summer's time;　5
The teeming Autumn, big with rich increase,
Bearing the wanton burthen of the prime,
Like widow'd wombs after their Lords' decease:
Yet this abundant issue seem'd to me
But crop of Orphans and unfather'd fruit;　10
For Summer and his pleasures wait on thee,
And, thou away, the very birds are mute;
　Or, if they sing, 'tis with so dull a cheer
　That leaves look pale, dreading the Winter's near.

Line 10, Q. reads 'But hope of Orphans'. The emendation is Staunton's.

Between the preceding sonnet and this one we are bound to infer an absence stretching over a considerable time. I conjecture that Mr. W.H., annoyed by Shakespeare's reproofs and moralizing, had completely deserted him for the time. This sonnet marks the reconciliation between the two friends. Butler reckons that the estrangement lasted about three or four months and he dates this sonnet 'Autumn 1586'. He further points out that there appears to be an interval of many months between the writing of this sonnet and the next 119 (98 Q.) 'for', he says, 'while 97 Q. implies Autumn 98 and 99, which follow in right order, *inter se*, imply Spring and early Summer.'

119 (98 Q.)

To Mr. W.H. Summer 1587.

From you have I been absent in the spring,
When proud-pi'd April, dress'd in all his trim,
Hath put a spirit of youth in everything,
That heavy *Saturn* laugh'd and leap'd with him.
Yet nor the lays of birds, nor the sweet smell   5
Of diff'rent flow'rs in odour and in hue,
Could make me any summer's story tell,
Or from their proud lap pluck them where they grew:
Nor did I wonder at the Lily's white,
Nor praise the deep vermilion in the Rose;   10
They were but, sweet, but figures of delight,
Drawn after you, you patterns of all those.
    Yet seem'd it Winter still, and, you away,
    As with your shadow I with these did play:

120 (99 Q.)

To Mr. W.H.
A continuation of the preceding sonnet.

The forward violet thus did I chide:
Sweet thief, whence didst thou steal thy sweet that
    smells,

If not from my love's breath? The purple pride
Which on thy soft cheek for complexion dwells
In my love's veins thou hast too grossly dyed.   5
The Lily I condemned for thy hand,
And buds of marjoram had stol'n thy hair;
The Roses fearfully on thorns did stand,
One blushing shame, another white despair;
A third, nor red nor white, had stol'n of both,   10
And to his robb'ry had annex'd thy breath;
But, for his theft, in pride of all his growth
A vengeful canker eat him up to death.
    More flow'rs I noted, yet I none could see
    But sweet or colour it had stol'n from thee.   15

This sonnet has an additional line after the fourth line,
which in the Shakespearian sonnet-form has no right
to be there. The result is that the sonnet has fifteen
lines instead of the regulation fourteen. The learned
commentators, not being poets, seem to take this quite
calmly, and scarcely notice the astonishing slip for
which I am convinced Shakespeare cannot have been
responsible. I can only suggest that in his MS. he had
roughly written out two suggested alternative lines,
meaning to suppress one of them and re-write the
other lines to fit. But he omitted to do this, and
Thorpe and his printers did not notice the blunder.

Line 9, Q. reads 'Our blushing shame'. The emendation is Malone's.

121 (100 Q.)

To Mr. W.H.
Following Butler, I date this sonnet Spring 1588.

Where art thou, Muse, that thou forget'st so long
To speak of that which gives thee all thy might?
Spend'st thou thy fury on some worthless song
Darkening thy pow'r to lend base subjects light!
Return, forgetful Muse, and straight redeem   5
In gentle numbers time so idly spent;
Sing to the ear that doth thy lays esteem
And gives thy pen both skill and argument.
Rise, resty Muse, my love's sweet face survey,
If Time have any wrinkle graven there;   10
If any, be a *satire* to decay,
And make Time's spoils despised every where:
    Give my love fame faster than Time wastes life;
    So thou prevent'st his scythe and crooked knife.

Lines 10 and 11. Butler writes: 'These lines suggest that Mr. W.H.'s good looks were beginning to go off.'

122 (101 Q.)

To Mr. W.H. A continuation of the preceding sonnet.

O Truant Muse, what shall be thy amends
For thy neglect of truth in beauty dy'd?
Both truth and beauty on my love depends;
So dost thou too, and therein dignifi'd.
Make answer, Muse: wilt thou not haply say,   5
'Truth needs no colour, with his colour fix'd;
Beauty no pencil, beauty's truth to lay;
But best is best, if never intermix'd'?
Because he needs no praise, wilt thou be dumb?
Excuse not silence so, for't lies in thee   10
To make him much outlive a gilded tomb
And to be prais'd of ages yet to be.
   Then do thy office, Muse; I teach thee how
   To make him seem long hence as he shows now.

123 (102 Q.)

To Mr. W.H.

My love is strengthen'd, though more weak in
   seeming;
I love not less, though less the show appear:
That love is merchandiz'd whose rich esteeming

The owner's tongue doth publish every where.
Our love was new and then but in the spring   5
When I was wont to greet it with my lays;
As *Philomel* in summer'd front doth sing
And stops her pipe in growth of riper days:
Not that the summer is less pleasant now
Than when her mournful hymns did hush the night, 10
But that wild music burthens every bough
And sweets grown common lose their dear delight.
   Therefore like her I sometime hold my tongue,
Because I would not dull you with my song.

Shakespeare here excuses himself for not writing so
many sonnets, so often, to his friend, but declares that
this is in no way due to any lessening of his love.

124 (103 Q.)

To Mr. W.H.

Alack, what poverty my Muse brings forth,
That having such a scope to show her pride,
The argument, all bare, is of more worth
Than when it hath my added praise beside!
O, blame me not, if I no more can write!   5
Look in your glass, and there appears a face

That over-goes my blunt invention quite,
Dulling my lines and doing me disgrace.
Were it not sinful then, striving to mend,
To mar the subject that before was well?   10
For to no other pass my verses tend
Than of your graces and your gifts to tell;
   And more, much more, than in my verse can sit,
   Your own glass shows you when you look in it.

125 (104 Q.)

To Mr. W.H.

To me, fair friend, you never can be old,
For as you were when first your eye I eyed,
Such seems your beauty still. Three winters cold
Have from the forests shook three summers' pride,
Three beauteous springs to yellow autumn turn'd   5
In process of the seasons have I seen,
Three April perfumes in three hot Junes burn'd,
Since first I saw you fresh, which yet are green.
Ah, yet doth beauty, like a dial-hand,
Steal from his figure, and no pace perceiv'd;   10
So your sweet hue, which still methinks doth stand,
Hath motion, and mine eye may be deceiv'd:

For fear of which, hear this, thou age unbred;
Ere you were born, was beauty's summer dead.

Line 11, Q. reads 'methinks still'. I venture to amend, as the words may have been misplaced by the printer.

This sonnet definitely settles the fact that Shakespeare's devotion to Mr. W.H. had now lasted three years.

Butler comments as follows: 'It would seem as though Mr. W.H. had been saying something to Shakespeare about his looking old. Shakespeare asseverates that to him he can never seem old, however much he may do so to other people. "Such seems your beauty still", gives an uncertain sound; so also do the last six lines.'

The reader is invited to note that if Mr. W.H. was eighteen when he first met Shakespeare (he may well have been a year or two younger, but hardly older considering the description of his appearance in the early sonnets) he would now be only twenty-one. Yet Shakespeare evidently thinks that this is an age when a young man is 'getting on' in years, and he finds it necessary to assure his friend that age had not yet begun to wither him. This supports my conviction, already insisted on more than once in this book, that

Shakespeare himself was very young when he wrote the Sonnets and that, in his estimation, at twenty-one youth was over. No doubt he changed his opinion on this subject as he grew older, but at the time he wrote the Sonnets, youth seemed to lie behind him.

126 (105 Q.)

To Mr. W.H.

Let not my love be call'd idolatry,
Nor my beloved as an Idol show,
Since all alike my songs and praises be
To one, of one, still such, and ever so.
Kind is my love to-day, to-morrow kind, 5
Still constant in a wondrous excellence;
Therefore my verse to constancy confin'd,
One thing expressing, leaves out difference.
'Fair, kind, and true', is all my argument,
'Fair, kind, and true', varying to other words; 10
And in this change is my invention spent,
Three themes in one, which wondrous scope affords.
 'Fair, kind, and true', have often lived alone,
 Which three till now never kept seat in one.

127 (106 Q.)

To Mr. W.H.

When in the chronicle of wasted time
I see descriptions of the fairest wights,
And beauty making beautiful old rhyme,
In praise of Ladies dead, and lovely Knights;
Then, in the blazon of sweet beauty's best,   5
Of hand, of foot, of lip, of eye, of brow,
I see their antique Pen would have express'd
Even such a beauty as you master now.
So all their praises are but prophecies
Of this our time, all you prefiguring;   10
And, for they look'd but with divining eyes,
They had not skill enough your worth to sing:
    For we, which now behold these present days,
    Have eyes to wonder, but lack tongues to praise.

Line 12, Q. reads 'still'. The emendation is Tyrwhitt's, adopted by Malone.

There does not seem much support in this superb
sonnet for Butler's suggestion that Mr. W.H. was
losing his looks!

128 (107 Q.)

To Mr. W.H. Reflecting the relief of the whole
nation at having passed through a time of great danger.
Dated by Butler 'About August 8, 1588'.

Not mine own fears, nor the prophetic soul
Of the wide world dreaming on things to come,
Can yet the lease of my true love control,
Supposed as forfeit to a confin'd doom.
The mortal Moon hath her eclipse endur'd,   5
And the sad Augurs mock their own presage;
Incertainties now crown themselves assur'd,
And peace proclaims Olives of endless age.
Now with the drops of this most balmy time
My love looks fresh, and Death to me subscribes, 10
Since, spite of him, I'll live in this poor rhyme,
While he insults o'er dull and speechless tribes:
   And thou in this shalt find thy monument,
   When tyrants' crests and tombs of brass are spent.

Line 4, 'confin'd = 'cònfin'd'.
This is the sonnet which, if one could be sure of the
public event to which it refers, would settle once for
all the date of the Sonnets. Sir Sydney Lee confidently
asserts that it was written in 1603 (!) and that it refers,
in a way that 'cannot be mistaken', to (1) Queen Eliza-

beth's death, (2) the accession of James I, and (3) the release from prison of the Earl of Southampton.

Butler comments as follows: 'I find it easy to avoid discovering reference to any one of the events mentioned by Mr. Lee as being referred to in a way "that cannot be mistaken". The death of Queen Elizabeth? To me the sonnet suggests that she was not only not dead, but had emerged from a time of apparent peril with splendour, all undimmed. "Cynthia (i.e., the moon), says Mr. Lee, "was the Queen's recognized poetic appellation"—No one will deny that Queen Elizabeth is intended by the words "The mortal moon", but not many will admit that Shakespeare would have compared her to the moon, and have said that she had "endured her eclipse", unless he meant to say that she had endured it as the moon endures it, and had passed from under the shadow with undiminished brightness.'

Butler goes on to make short work of Sir Sydney Lee's conclusions as to the supposed references in the sonnet to the accession of James I and the release of Southampton from prison. I cannot quote him at length, but I can assert that he pulverizes Sir Sydney Lee's assumptions, and I refer my readers to his book.

Butler confidently declares that Shakespeare's reference is to the defeat of the Armada, which became known in the first days of August 1588. He clinches his argument by an extract from *Stow's Annals*, which gives an account of the Queen's procession to St. Paul's in November 1588 to render thanks for the great victory, on which occasion 'Her Majesty having attendant upon her the Privy Council and Nobility, and other honourable persons as well as spiritual and temporal in great number, the French Ambassador, the Judges of the Realme, the heralds, trumpeters, and all on horseback, did come in a chariot-throne made with four pillars behind, to have a canopy, on the top whereof was made a crown imperial, and two lower pillars before, whereon stood a Lion and a Dragon, supporters of the Arms of England, drawn by two white horses from Somerset House to the Cathedral Church of St. Paul, her footmen and pensioners about her. . . .'

In Sonnet 148 (125 Q.) Shakespeare has the following, which Butler takes to be a reference to this canopy which Shakespeare (as one of the Queen's footmen or pensioners) helped to bear:

'Were't aught to me I bore the canopy
With my extern the outward honouring.'

I accept all this as conclusive, and I believe that this fixes the dates of the sonnets as beginning in Spring

1585 and concluding with the sonnet about the Canopy in November 1588. The Canopy Sonnet, according to Butler's reckoning, the accuracy of which I think he has established, is the last sonnet in the W.H. series.

129 (108 Q.)

To Mr. W.H.

What's in the brain, that ink may character,
Which hath not figur'd to thee my true spirit?
What's new to speak, what new to register,
That may express my love, or thy dear merit?
Nothing, sweet boy; but yet, like prayers divine, 5
I must each day say o'er the very same;
Counting no old thing old, thou mine, I thine,
Even as when first I hallow'd thy fair name,
So that eternal love in love's fresh case
Weighs not the dust and injury of age, 10
Nor gives to necessary wrinkles place,
But makes antiquity for aye his page;
    Finding the first conceit of love there bred,
      Where time and outward form would show it dead.

George Wyndham says of this sonnet: 'I am convinced that the Poet does *not* refer to any change in the outward beauty of the Friend'.

130 (109 Q.)

A continuation of the preceding sonnet.

O, never say that I was false of heart,
Though absence seem'd my flame to qualify!
As easy might I from myself depart,
As from my soul, which in thy breast doth lie:
That is my home of love: if I have rang'd,   5
Like him that travels, I return again,
Just to the time, not with the time exchang'd,
So that myself bring water for my stain.
Never believe, though in my nature reign'd
All frailties that besiege all kinds of blood,   10
That it could so prepost'rously be stain'd,
To leave for nothing all thy sum of good;
   For nothing this wide Universe I call,
   Save thou, my Rose; in it thou art my all.

131 (110 Q.)

To Mr. W.H.

Alas, 'tis true I have gone here and there,
And made myself a motley to the view,
Gor'd mine own thoughts, sold cheap what is most
   dear,

Made old offences of affections new;
Most true it is that I have look'd on truth   5
Askance and strangely; but, by all above,
These blenches gave my heart another youth,
And worse essays prov'd thee my best of love.
Now all is done, save what shall have no end:
Mine appetite I never more will grind   10
On newer proof, to try an older friend,
A God in love, to whom I am confin'd,
  Then give me welcome, next my heav'n the best,
  Even to thy pure and most most loving breast.

Line 9, Q. reads: 'have what shall have no end'. The
emendation is Tyrwhitt's, adopted by Malone.

132 (110 Q.)

To Mr. W.H.

O, for my sake do you with fortune chide,
The guilty goddess of my harmful deeds,
That did not better for my life provide
Than public means, which public manners breeds.
Thence comes it that my name receives a brand;   5
And almost thence my nature is subdu'd
To what it works in like the Dyer's hand:

Pity me, then, and wish I were renew'd:
Whilst, like a willing patient, I will drink
Potions of Eisel 'gainst my strong infection;   10
No bitterness that I will bitter think,
Nor double penance, to correct correction.
    Pity me, then, dear friend, and I assure ye,
    Even that your pity is enough to cure me.

Line 1, Q. reads, 'doe you wish fortune chide'. The
emendation is Malone's.

133 (112 Q.)

To Mr. W.H.

Your love and pity doth the impression fill
Which vulgar scandal stamp'd upon my brow;
For what care I who calls me well or ill,
So you o'er-green my bad, my good allow?
You are my All the world, and I must strive   5
To know my shames and praises from your tongue;
None else to me, nor I to none alive,
That my steel'd sense or changes right or wrong,
In so profound *Abysm* I throw all care
Of others' voices, that my Adder's sense.   10

194

To critic and to flatt'rer stopped are.
Mark how with my neglect I do dispense:
    You are so strongly in my purpose bred
    That all the world besides methinks are dead.

Line 14. Q. reads: 'That all the world beside me thinkes y'are dead'. This is Malone's emendation.

134 (113 Q.)

To Mr. W.H., written while travelling.

Since I left you mine eye is in my mind,
And that which governs me to go about
Doth part his function and is partly blind,
Seems seeing, but effectually is out;
For it no form delivers to the heart   5
Of bird, of flow'r, or shape, which it doth latch:
Of his quick object hath the mind no part,
Nor his own vision holds what it doth catch;
For if it see the rud'st or gentlest sight,
The most sweet favour or deformed'st creature, 10
The mountain or the sea, the day or night,
The Crow or Dove, it shapes them to your feature:
    Incapable of more, replete with you,
    My most true mind thus maketh mine untrue.

Line 6, Q. reads 'lack'. The emendation is Malone's, who explains that 'to latch' formerly meant to 'lay hold of'.

Line 14: 'Untrue' here is substantive and ='untruth', as Malone points out. The sense is: 'The trueness (loyalty) of my mind to you has the effect of creating my false perceptions.'

135 (114 Q.)

To Mr. W.H.

Or whether doth my mind, being crown'd with you,
Drink up the monarch's plague, this flattery?
Or whether shall I say, mine eye saith true,
And that your love taught it this *Alchemy*,
To make of monsters and things indigest   5
Such cherubins as your sweet self resemble,
Creating every bad a perfect best,
As fast as objects to his beams assemble?
O, 'tis the first; 'tis flattery in my seeing,
And my great mind most kingly drinks it up: 10
Mine eye well knows what with his gust is 'greeing,
And to his palate doth prepare the cup:

If it be poison'd, 'tis the lesser sin
That mine eye loves it, and doth first begin.

136 (115 Q.)

To Mr. W.H.

Those lines that I before have writ do lie,
Even those that said I could not love you dearer.
Yet then my judgment knew no reason why
My most full flame should afterwards burn clearer.
But reckoning time, whose million'd accidents   5
Creep in 'twixt vows, and change decrees of kings,
Tan sacred beauty, blunt the sharp'st intents,
Divert strong minds to the course of alt'ring things;
Alas, why, fearing of Time's tyranny,
Might I not then say 'Now I love you best',   10
When I was certain o'er incertainty,
Crowning the present, doubting of the rest?
    Love is a babe; then might I not say so,
    To give full growth to that which still doth grow?

Line 8. This line is a syllable too long. It would be
put right by omitting the word 'the', thus:
    'Divert strong minds to course of alt'ring things.'

137 (116 Q.)
To Mr. W.H.

Let me not to the marriage of true minds
Admit impediments. Love is not love
Which alters when it alteration finds,
Or bends with the remover to remove:
O no! it is an ever-fixed mark   5
That looks on tempests and is never shaken;
It is the star to every wand'ring bark,
Whose worth's unknown, although his height be
    taken.
Love's not Time's fool, though rosy lips and cheeks
Within his bending sickle's compass come;   10
Love alters not with his brief hours and weeks,
But bears it out even to the edge of doom.
    If this be error and upon me proved,
    I never writ, nor no man ever loved.

Butler's sub-heading to this magnificent sonnet is as follows: 'To Mr. W.H., who has been again upbraiding the writer and making the continuation of the old friendship difficult,' which strikes me as being as unwarrantable, and as unfair to Mr. W.H., as it possibly could be. Once more I suspect that Butler is thinking of the perfidious Pauli, whom in his mind he almost identifies with Shakespeare's friend.

138 (117 Q.)

To Mr. W.H.

Accuse me thus: that I have scanted all
Wherein I should your great deserts repay.
Forgot upon your dearest love to call,
Whereto all bonds do tie me day by day;
That I have frequent been with unknown minds, 5
And given to them your own dear-purchas'd right;
That I have hoisted sail to all the winds
Which should transport me farthest from your sight.
Book both my wilfulness and errors down,
And on just proof surmise accumulate; 10
Bring me within the level of your frown,
But shoot not at me in your waken'd hate;
    Since my appeal says I did strive to prove
    The constancy and virtue of your love.

Line 6, Quarto: 'and given to time'. The emendation
is Staunton's.

139 (118 Q.)

To Mr. W.H., a continuation of the preceding sonnet.

Like as, to make our appetites more keen,
With eager compounds we our palate urge;

As, to prevent our maladies unseen,
We sicken, to shun sickness, when we purge:
Even so, being full of your ne'er-cloying sweetness, 5
To bitter sauces did I frame my feeding,
And, sick of welfare, found a kind of meetness
To be diseas'd ere that there was true needing.
Thus policy in love, t'anticipate
The ills that were not, grew to faults assur'd;   10
And brought to medicine a healthful state,
Which, rank of goodness, would by ill be cur'd:
   But thence I learn, and find the lesson true,
   Drugs poison him that so fell sick of you.

140 (147 Q.)

To Mr. W.H. (?)

My love is as a fever, longing still
For that which longer nurseth the disease;
Feeding on that which doth preserve the ill,
The uncertain sickly appetite to please.
My reason, the Physician to my love,   5
Angry that his prescriptions are not kept,
Hath left me, and I desp'rate now approve
Desire is death, which Physic did except.
Past cure I am, now Reason is past care,

And frantic-mad with evermore unrest;　　　10
My thoughts and my discourse as madmen's are,
At random from the truth vainly express'd;
　For I have sworn thee fair, and thought thee
　　bright,
Who art as black as hell, as dark as night.

Butler whose order I have followed so far with only
two variations, puts this sonnet and the three following
in this place. He says: 'I may be speculating too
boldly, but I imagine that Mr. W.H., not too well
pleased at the excuses made in 117 Q. and 118 Q.,
said things to Shakespeare in return which outraged
him not a little, and that Shakespeare in the heat of
anger and passionate regret, wrote the four sonnets
147-150 Q., which Thorpe excluded from the first
group, and which I have restored to what I believe
to have been their proper place.'

I am not at all convinced that these sonnets are
rightly placed. I more than half believe that they apply
to the 'dark woman' and should be left in the 'dark
woman' group where they were placed by Thorpe.
Butler admits that he 'may be speculating too boldly'.
His violent *parti pris* against Mr. W.H. has been exhibited all through, and this may be another instance
of it. I incline to think it is, and I leave the sonnets in

this place only tentatively. I cannot fit the violence and bitterness of these sonnets into the picture, if they are taken as addressed to Mr. W.H. Whereas there are many admittedly addressed to the 'dark woman' which are much in the same vein as these.

141 (148 Q.)

To Mr. W.H. (?)

O Me, what eyes hath Love put in my head
Which have no correspondence with true sight.
Or, if they have, where is my judgment fled,
That censures falsely what they see aright?
If that be fair whereon my false eyes dote,   5
What means the world to say it is not so?
If it be not, then love doth well denote
Love's 'eye' is not so true as all men's 'no':
How can it? O, how can Love's eye be true,
That is so vex'd with watching and with tears?   10
No marvel then, though I mistake my view;
The sun itself sees not till heaven clears.
    O cunning love! with tears thou keep'st me blind,
    Lest eyes well-seeing thy foul faults should find.

142 (149 Q.)

To Mr. W.H. (?)

Canst thou, O cruel! say I love thee not,
When I against myself with thee partake?
Do I not think on thee, when I forgot
Am of myself, all tyrant, for thy sake?
Who hateth thee that I do call my friend?   5
On whom frown'st thou that I do fawn upon?
Nay, if thou lour'st on me, do I not spend
Revenge upon myself with present moan?
What merit do I in myself respect,
That is so proud thy service to despise,   10
When all my best doth worship thy defect,
Commanded by the motion of thine eyes?
    But, love, hate on, for now I know thy mind;
    Those that can see thou lov'st, and I am blind.

143 (150 Q.)

To Mr. W.H. (?)

O, from what power hast thou this powerful might,
With insufficiency my heart to sway?
To make me give the lie to my true sight,

And swear that brightness doth not grace the day?
Whence hast thou this becoming of things ill,   5
That in the very refuse of thy deeds
There is such strength and warrantise of skill,
That, in my mind, thy worst all best exceeds?
Who taught thee how to make me love thee more,
The more I hear and see just cause of hate?   10
O, though I love what others do abhor,
With others thou shouldst not abhor my state:
   If thy unworthiness rais'd love in me,
   More worthy I to be belov'd of thee.

144 (119 Q.)

To Mr. W.H.

What potions have I drunk of Siren tears,
Distill'd from limbecks foul as hell within,
Applying fears to hopes and hopes to fears,
Still losing when I saw myself to win!
What wretched errors hath my heart committed,   5
Whilst it hath thought itself so blessed never!
How have mine eyes out of their spheres been fitted,
In the distraction of this madding fever!
O benefit of ill! now I find true

That better is by evil still made better;   10
And ruin'd love, when it is built anew,
Grows fairer than at first, more strong, far greater.
  So I return rebuked to my content,
  And gain by ill thrice more than I have spent.

145 (120 Q.)

To Mr. W.H.

That you were once unkind befriends me now,
And for that sorrow which I then did feel
Needs must I under my transgression bow,
Unless my nerves were brass or hammer'd steel.
For if you were by my unkindness shaken   5
As I by yours, you've passed a hell of Time,
And I, a tyrant, have no leisure taken
To weigh how once I suffer'd in your crime.
O that our night of woe might have remember'd
My deepest sense, how hard true sorrow hits,   10
And soon to you, as you to me, then tender'd
The humble salve which wounded bosoms fits!
  But that your trespass now becomes a fee;
  Mine ransoms yours, and yours must ransom me.

146 (122 Q.)

To Mr. W.H., who has reproached the Poet for having given away a present of tablets which Mr. W.H. had made him.

Thy gift, thy tables, are within my brain
Full character'd with lasting memory,
Which shall above that idle rank remain,
Beyond all date, even to eternity:
Or, at the least, so long as brain and heart   5
Have faculty by nature to subsist;
Till each to raz'd oblivion yield his part
Of thee, thy record never can be miss'd.
That poor retention could not so much hold,
Nor need I tallies thy dear love to score;   10
Therefore to give them from me was I bold,
To trust those tables that receive thee more:
    To keep an adjunct to remember thee
    Were to import forgetfulness in me.

147 (123 Q.)

To Mr. W.H.

No, Time, thou shalt not boast that I do change:
Thy pyramids built up with newer might

To me are nothing novel, nothing strange;
They are but dressings of a former sight.
Our dates are brief, and therefore we admire   5
What thou dost foist upon us that is old;
And rather make them bourne to our desire
Than think that we before have heard them told.
Thy registers and thee I both defy,
Not wond'ring at the present nor the past,   10
For thy records and what we see doth lie,
Made more or less by thy continual haste.
   This I do vow, and this shall ever be,
   I will be true, despite thy scythe and thee.

Line 7, Q. reads 'borne to our desire'. I accept
George Wyndham's emendation.
Line 11, 'records' = 'recòrds'.

148 (124 Q.)

To Mr. W.H.

If my dear love were but the child of state,
It might for fortune's bastard be unfather'd,
As subject to time's love or to time's hate,
Weeds among weeds, or flow'rs with flowers
    gather'd.

No, it was builded far from accident;   5
It suffers not in smiling pomp, nor falls
Under the blow of thralled discontent,
Whereto the inviting time or fashion calls:
It fears not policy, that *Heretic*,
Which works on leases of short-number'd hours, 10
But all alone stands hugely politic,
That it nor grows with heat nor drowns with show'rs.
    To this I witness call the souls of time,
      Which die for goodness, who have lived for
      crime.

Line 8, Q. reads, 'our fashion calls'. The emendation is Capell's.

Line 13, Q. reads, 'foles of time'. Butler supposes this to be a misprint for 'soles'. I adopt his emendation.

149 (125 Q.)

To Mr. W.H. (the last sonnet).
Probably written at the end of 1588.

Were't aught to me I bore the canopy,
With my extern the outward honouring,
Or laid great bases for eternity,
Which prove more short than waste or ruining?

Have I not seen dwellers on form and favour   5
Lose all, and more, by paying too much rent
For compound sweet; forgoing simple savour,
Pitiful thrivers, in their gazing spent?
No, let me be obsequious in thy heart,
And take thou my oblation, poor but free,   10
Which is not mix'd with seconds, knows no art
But mutual renders, only me for thee.
    Hence, thou suborn'd *Informer!* a true soul
    When most impeach'd stands least in thy control.

This is the sonnet about the canopy already referred
to in my remarks on sonnet 128 (107 Q.).

Lines 13 and 14. It is impossible to reconcile the
violence and contempt of the two concluding lines
with the rest of the sonnet. Butler describes this
sonnet thus: 'To Mr. W.H. After another and probably final rupture.' But we cannot be at all sure that
the friendship came to an end with this sonnet. No
more sonnets belonging to the series exist, it is true,
as far as we know; but it would be very rash to assume,
even if we could make head or tail of the phrase about
the 'suborn'd Informer', and even if we were certain
that it is meant for Mr. W.H. that Shakespeare and
he did not 'make it up' again.

Butler comments as follows: 'In this last sonnet

there is a reference to the bearing of a certain canopy, apparently on some very great occasion, over some great personage: Shakespeare seems either to have had some part in the bearing of this canopy, which had given rise to ill-natured remarks, or else to have been maliciously foiled in an attempt to be included among the bearers; on the whole, I should say, the second interpretation of Shakespeare's words is the more probable.' Accepting this interpretation of the sonnet, one is almost constrained to accept also the application of the words 'suborn'd *Informer*' to Mr. W.H.

But on the other hand George Wyndham has the following; ' "Hence thou suborned *Informer*". I have argued elsewhere that the words in italics with capitals are not accidents of printing. This word of violent apostrophe refers to some person whose identity was obvious to the subject of Shakespeare's verse, and if, as I have tried to show, these sonnets belong to one sequence, it may be compared to the "frailer spies" of 121 (Q.).'

If we adopt Wyndham's explanation of this very obscure sonnet, we must assume that the words 'Hence thou suborn'd *Informer*' are not directed at Mr. W.H. at all. In that case this sonnet, though the last of the series, would not imply any 'final rupture', as Butler calls it, or any rupture at all, between Shakespeare and Mr. W.H. I incline to this second view, because, as I have already said, it is quite impossible to reconcile the violence and contempt of the two concluding lines, if they are meant for Mr. W.H., with the affectionate and humble tone of lines of 9 and 10.

I see nothing whatever in the text of the sonnets to support Butler's furious attack on the character of Mr. W.H. Being unafflicted with a Pauli complex, and being, moreover, very sure in my own mind that Shakespeare would not have loved Will Hughes so much unless he had had something more than his good looks to commend him, I see no reason at all to accept Butler's estimate of his character or of his influence on Shakespeare.

There is nothing whatever to prevent us from supposing that he and Shakespeare went on being friends as long as they were both alive; and I, for my part, shall continue to keep in my heart a warm and grateful remembrance of the wonderful boy who inspired the greatest of all poets to write a great deal of his loveliest poetry.

Appendix I (146 Q.)

An occasional sonnet probably given to Mr. W.H.
but having no reference to him.

Poor soul, the centre of my sinful earth,
Starv'd by these rebel powers that thee array,
Why dost thou pine within and suffer dearth,
Painting thy outward walls so costly gay?
Why so large cost, having so short a lease, 5
Dost thou upon thy fading mansion spend?
Shall worms, inheritors of this excess,
Eat up thy charge? is this thy body's end?
Then, soul, live thou upon thy servant's loss,
And let that pine to aggravate thy store; 10
Buy terms divine in selling hours of dross;
Within be fed, without be rich no more:
So shalt thou feed on death, that feeds on men,
And death once dead, there's no more dying then.

Line 2, Quarto reads: 'My sinful earth these rebel
powers that thee array', which is obviously corrupt.
The emendation by Steevens which I have adopted is
purely conjectural, and it is very improbable that it is
exactly what Shakespeare wrote. The Temple edition
prints the line thus:

'. . . these rebel powers that thee obey.'

It is very unfortunate that this splendid sonnet revealing, as it does, Shakespeare's deeply religious soul, should suffer by the mutilation of the second line. Massey's emendation, quoted with approval by George Wyndham, is:

'My sinful earth these rebel powers array.'

Wyndham says, 'it has the merit of adding nothing to the text and of restoring euphony to one of the finest among Shakespeare's sonnets'. Wyndham goes on to point out that there is warrant in other sonnets for repeating the last words of a preceding line. This is, indeed, a well-known and effective poetical device, e.g. Sonnet 142 Q.:

'Love is my sin, and thy dear virtue hate,
Hate of my sin, grounded on sinful loving.'

All the same, I prefer Steevens's conjecture.

Appendix II (145 Q.)

A sonnet in Octosyllabic lines, probably a translation.
It has no relation to the Sonnet series.

Those lips that Love's own hand did make
Breath'd forth the sound that said 'I hate',

To me that languish'd for her sake:
But when she saw my woeful state,
Straight in her heart did mercy come,   5
Chiding that tongue that ever sweet
Was us'd in giving gentle doom;
And taught it thus anew to greet;
'I hate' she alter'd with an end,
That follow'd it as gentle day   10
Doth follow night, who, like a fiend,
From heaven to hell is flown away;
  'I hate' from hate away she threw
  And sav'd my life, saying 'not you'.

I feel pretty certain that this feeble stuff is not by Shakespeare, and how it got into the Quarto I cannot imagine. I leave it here, but I definitely reject it as spurious.

If it be said that I am now doing what I have condemned in Mr. J. M. Robertson, I reply that it is quite possible to believe that one spurious poem may have somehow crept into Thorpe's collection. It is quite another thing to reject a whole mass of the Sonnets, including some of the finest, as Mr. Robertson does.

Appendix III (153 Q.)

A sonnet based on a Latin version of a Greek Epigram
by Byzantine Marianus.

Cupid laid by his brand and fell asleep:
A maid of *Dian's* this advantage found,
And his love-kindling fire did quickly steep
In a cold valley-fountain of that ground;
Which borrow'd from this holy fire of Love   5
A dateless lively heat, still to endure,
And grew a seething bath, which yet men prove
Against strange maladies a sovereign cure.
But at my mistress' eye Love's brand new-fired,
The boy for trial needs would touch my breast;   10
I, sick withal, the help of bath desired,
And thither hied, a sad distemper'd guest,
    But found no cure: the bath for my help lies
    Where *Cupid* got new fire, my mistress' eyes.

Although this is a very poor sonnet, I would not care
to say that it is not by Shakespeare. Shakespeare, like
all other poets (though perhaps less than any other
poet), is not by any means always up to his own best
standard.

Appendix IV (154 Q.)

This is simply another, and improved, version of the
preceding sonnet.

The little Love-God, lying once asleep,
Laid by his side his heart-inflaming brand,
Whilst many nymphs that vow'd chaste life to keep,
Came tripping by; but in her maiden hand
The fairest votary took up that fire   5
Which many Legions of true hearts had warm'd;
And so the General of hot desire
Was, sleeping, by a Virgin hand disarm'd.
This brand she quenched in a cool Well by,
Which from Love's fire took heat perpetual,   10
Growing a bath and healthful remedy
For men diseas'd; but I, my Mistress' thrall,
    Came there for cure, and this by that I prove,
    Love's fire heats water, water cools not love.